The First Afghan War

The First Afghan War

A Brief Sketch 1839-1842

Mowbray Morris

LEONAUR

The First Afghan War
A Brief Sketch 1839-1842
by Mowbray Morris

First published under the title
The First Afghan War

Leonaur is an imprint
of Oakpast Ltd

Copyright in this form © 2010 Oakpast Ltd

ISBN: 978-0-85706-347-2 (hardcover)
ISBN: 978-0-85706-348-9 (softcover)

http://www.leonaur.com

Publisher's Notes

The opinions of the authors represent a view of events in which he
was a participant related from his own perspective,
as such the text is relevant as an historical document.

The views expressed in this book are not necessarily
those of the publisher.

Contents

Preface

The following pages pretend to give nothing more than a short summary of events already recorded by recognised authorities.

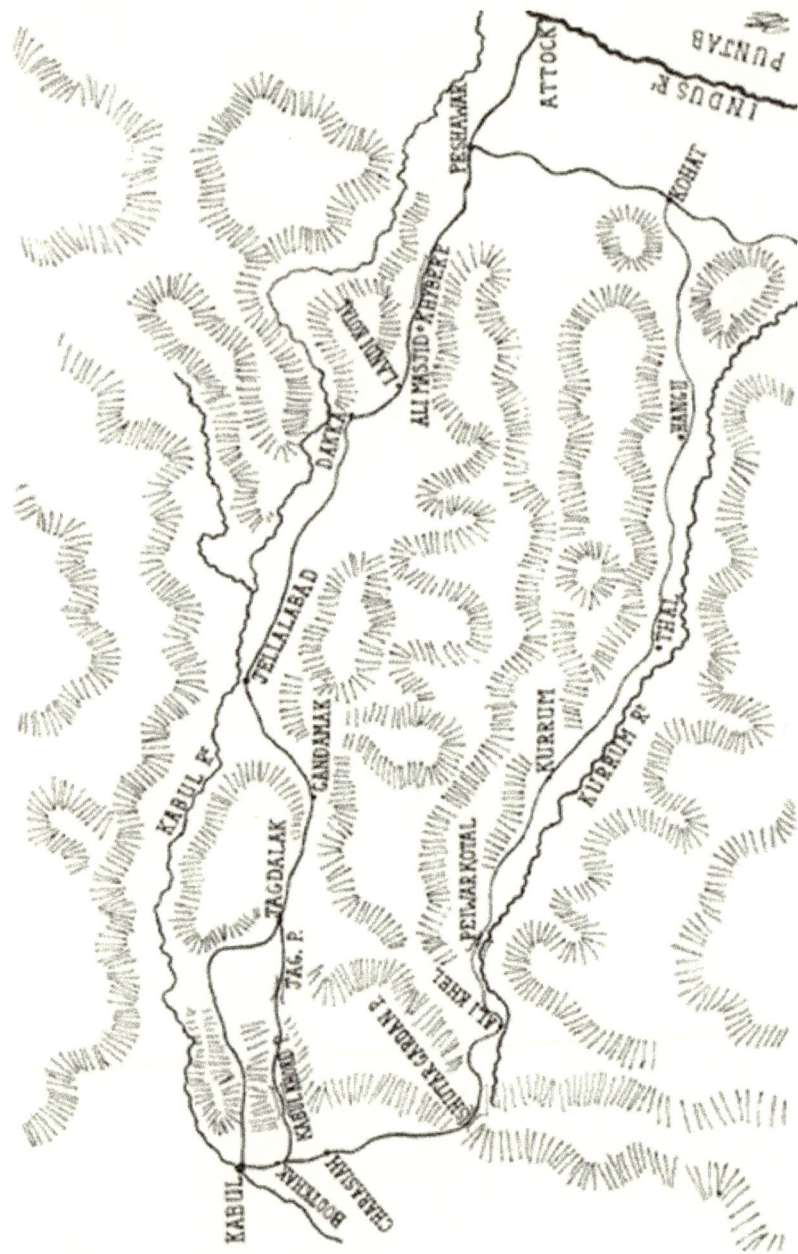

ROUTE–TAKEN–BY–KABUL–GARRISON–AND–RETREAT–1842

Map labels: PUNJAB, INDUS R⁻, ATTOCK, KOHAT, PESHAWAR, KHYBER, ALI MASJID, LANDI KOTAL, DAKKA, HANGI, JELLALABAD, GANDAMAK, KURRUM R, KURRUM, THAL, PEIWAR KOTAL, ALI KHEL, JAGDALAK, JAG. P., KABUL R, SUFFED CARDIN P, KABULKHO, BOOTKHAK, CHARASIAH, KABUL

The First Afghan War

It was in the year 1808, when the power of Napoleon was at its height, that diplomatic relations were first opened between the Courts of Calcutta and Cabul. Napoleon, when in Egypt, had meditated on the chances of striking a fatal blow at England through her Indian dependencies; some correspondence had actually passed between him and Tippoo Saib on the subject, and subsequently, in 1801, he had concluded a treaty with the Russian Emperor Paul for an invasion of India by a force of 70,000 men, to be composed of equal parts of French and Russian troops.

The proposed line of march was to lie through Astrakhan and Afghanistan to the Indus, and was to be heralded by Zemaun Shah, who then ruled at Cabul, at the head of 100,000 Afghans. There was but little danger indeed to be apprehended from Afghanistan alone, but Afghanistan with Russia and France in the background was capable of proving a very troublesome enemy. In such circumstances the attitude of Persia was of the last importance, and Marquess Wellesley, then Viceroy of India, at once proceeded to convert a possible enemy into a certain and valuable ally.

A young officer who had distinguished himself under Harris at Seringapatam was selected for this delicate service. How the young captain, whom Englishmen remember as Sir John Malcolm, fulfilled his mission is matter of history. A thorough master of all Oriental languages, and as skilful in council as he was brave in the field, Malcolm soon pledged the Court of Persia to the interests of England, and not only was it agreed that the two contracting parties should unite to expel any French force that might seek to gain a footing on any of the islands or shores of Persia, but the latter Government bound itself to "slay and disgrace" any Frenchman found in the country. This treaty, which may be thought to have somewhat dangerously stretched the bounds of diplomatic hostility, was, however, never formally ratified, and internal dissensions, culminating in the deposition of Zemaun Shah by his brother Mahmoud, removed all danger from our frontier for a time.

But the idea still lived in Napoleon's restless heart. The original treaty with Paul was discussed with his successor Alexander, and in 1808 a French mission, with the avowed design of organizing the proposed invasion, was despatched, not to Cabul, but to Teheran. The magic of Napoleon's name was stronger even than British eloquence and British gold, and Malcolm, once all-powerful in Iran, when he sought to renew the former pledges of amity, was turned back with insult from the Persian capital. A second mission, however, despatched direct from London under the guidance of Sir Harford Jones, was more fortunate.

Napoleon had been defeated in Spain, and the news of his defeat had spread. Russia was something less eager for the French alliance than she had been in 1801, while between the Muscovites and the Persians there had long existed a hereditary feud, which the proposed league had by no means served to extinguish. The English envoy, skilfully piecing together these broken threads to his own ends, was enabled with little loss of time to conclude an offensive and defensive alliance between Great Britain and Persia, the earliest result of which was the immediate dismissal of the French mission.

By this treaty the Persian King bound himself not to permit the passage through his dominions of any force hostile to India, and, in the event of war arising between England and Afghanistan, to invade the latter at the cost of the former; furthermore, he declared null all treaties previously concluded by him with any other European power. The English, in their turn, pledged themselves to assist him, should his kingdom be invaded, either with men or money and arms, but should the war be one only with Afghanistan, they were not to interfere unless their interference was sought by both parties. Though this treaty was concluded in 1808-9, it was not formally ratified till November 15, 1814.

Not on Persia alone, however, was the English Government content to rely. In a friendly Afghanistan was a second most serviceable string which it had been the height of imprudence to let another fit to his bow. The two countries stood in almost precisely similar relations to English India; each as an enemy contemptible single-handed, but a dangerous item in an invading force; each a useful ally, and each a salutary check upon the other. At the same time, then, as Sir Harford Jones was neutralizing the French influence at Teheran, the Honourable Mountstuart Elphinstone was despatched by Lord Minto, who had succeeded Lord Wellesley at Calcutta, to the Court of Cabul.

Previous to the year 1808 Afghanistan was practically a *terra incognita* to Englishmen. Zemaun Shah, the once terrible *Ameer* whose threatened invasion had disturbed even the strong mind of Lord Wellesley, was, indeed, in their hands, living, dethroned and blinded, a pensioner on their bounty at Loodhianah, but of the country he had once ruled over and of the subjects who had driven him into exile but little was known in Calcutta and still less in London.

Before the close of the eighteenth century but one Englishman had ever penetrated into that unknown land. Forster, a member of the Bengal Civil Service, in 1783-84 had crossed the Punjab to Cashmere, and thence had descended through the great Khyber and Koord-Cabul passes to the Afghan stronghold, whence journeying on by Ghuznee, Candahar, and Herat he had won his way to the borders of the Caspian Sea. His book was not published till some fifteen years after, and shows chiefly, to use Kaye's words, "how much during the last seventy years the Afghan Empire and how little the Afghan character is changed." But the labour and intelligence of one man, however much they may profit himself, have rarely by themselves added much to the knowledge of a nation.

Many well-read Englishmen could still own to little more than a vague idea of Afghanistan; that it was a bare and rocky country, which the heat of summer and the cold of winter alike rendered impervious to travellers, happily shut out from more civilised regions by a mighty barrier of mountains, topped with eternal snow, through which, by passes inaccessible to all save the mountaineers themselves, hordes of savage warriors had in earlier days poured down in irresistible flood on the fertile valleys of the Indus. Elphinstone let in more light on the gloomy and mysterious scene. Though with his own eyes he saw but little of the country and the people, as his journey was stayed at Peshawur, he acquired from various sources a vast amount of information, which he reproduced with extraordinary distinctness.

His book rapidly became the acknowledged text-book of the history and geography of the country, and may still be read with pleasure and studied with profit. It would have been well if one of the lessons he taught had been better laid to heart; and thirty years later his unfortunate namesake must have recalled with peculiar bitterness all he had once read of the ingrained treachery of the Afghan character. The mission was in itself entirely successful, though the rapid march of events soon neutralised, and eventually wholly destroyed its work. Shah Soojah, a name to be before many years but too familiar to English ears, received the envoys at Peshawur, then one of the chief cities of his kingdom.

He appeared to them in royal state, seated on a golden throne, and blazing with jewels, chief among which shone forth in a gorgeous bracelet the mighty Koh-i-noor. Nor were the English outdone in magnificence. The entire mission was on a scale of profuse splendour, and the presents they brought with them so numerous and so costly that when, thirty years later, Burnes arrived in Cabul the courtiers turned in disgust from what Kaye contemptuously calls "his pins and needles, and little articles of hardware, such as would have disgraced the wallet of a pedlar of low repute." The envoys were most hospitably received, and Elphinstone formed a very favourable opinion of the character of Soojah, whom he described as both affable and dignified and bearing the "manners of a gentleman."

He listened attentively to the envoys' proposals, and declared that "England and Cabul were designed by the Creator to be united by bonds of everlasting friendship," but at the same time he confessed his country to be in such an unsettled condition, and his own throne so insecure, that, for the present, the best advice he could give the English gentlemen was that they should retire beyond the frontier.

On June 14th, 1809, therefore, the mission set out on its homeward journey, having, however, arranged a treaty, which was shortly after formally ratified by Lord Minto at Calcutta, by which Soojah bound himself to treat the French, if allied with the Persians, much as the Persian monarch had pledged himself to behave to them if allied with the Afghans. But even at the very time of ratification this treaty had been practically rendered null by the success of Sir Harford Jones's mission to Teheran, and within a year Soojah had been deposed by his brother Mahmoud, from whom he had himself wrested the crown, and was a captive in the hands of Runjeet Singh.

The final overthrow of Napoleon in 1815 removed all fears of a French advance on India, but in its stead arose the still more imminent shadow of Russia. For many years past that shadow had been looming larger and larger to the eyes of the kings of Teheran, till the annexation of Georgia brought the eagles of the *Czar* over the Caucasus up to the very frontier of their northern provinces. The English alliance, and an army drilled under the supervision of English officers, had, however, turned the head of the Persian king, and his heir. Abbas Mirza, at the head of 40,000 troops, of whom half were drilled and equipped after the English fashion, dared, in 1826, to throw down the gauntlet to the *Czar*.

He paid dearly for his daring. English drill and English arms availed him little without English officers. His son, Mahomed

Mirza, was utterly routed with the division under his command, and soon after he himself was defeated in open battle by the Russian Paskewitch with a loss of 1200 men. The English help, promised by the treaty of 1814 in the event of Persia becoming involved in war with any European power, was not forthcoming. Mediation took the place of armed men, and with the help of Great Britain a peace was concluded in 1828 between the two powers, humiliating to Persia, and ultimately disastrous to England.

By this treaty Persia lost the Khanates of Erivan and Nakhichevan, and practically her whole defensive frontier to the north. In Sir Harford Jones's words, "Persia was delivered, bound hand and foot, to the Court of St. Petersburg." The territory acquired by Russia was nearly equal in extent to the whole of England, and her outposts were brought within a few days' march of the Persian capital. From that time, up to Lord Auckland's arrival at Calcutta in 1836, Persia was little more than a minion of the *Czar*, used by him to cover the steady advance of his battalions eastward.

The death of Futteh Ali Shah, at Ispahan in 1834, snapped the last link that bound Persia to our interests. Futteh Ali, as far as lay in his power, had ever striven to remain faithful to his English allies, and to resist, as far as he dared, Russian intrigue and Russian influence within his kingdom. But his son and grandson had welcomed the Muscovite alliance with open arms, and when the latter ascended the throne on his grandfather's death, it was evident that the *Czar* would be paramount at the Persian Court. Mahomed Mirza Shah, the new king, had long dreamed of the conquest of Herat and the extension of his eastern frontier, and had more than once, in his grandfather's lifetime, striven to turn his dreams to facts.

Nothing could have been more favourable to the Russian plans, and no sooner was Mahomed secure upon the throne than he was urged to the immediate execution of his long-cherished designs. Such was the state of affairs when Lord Auckland was despatched by Lord Melbourne in 1836 to take the reins of Indian Government from the hands of Sir Charles Metcalfe. Meanwhile many changes had taken place at Cabul. The weak and dissolute Mahmoud, the deposer of Soojah, proved no more than a puppet in the hands of his *Vizier*, Futteh Khan, the head of the great Barukzye tribe. The youngest of the twenty brothers of this able and powerful chief was the celebrated Dost Mahomed. Born of a woman of an inferior tribe, he had entered life as a sweeper of the sacred tomb of Lamech.

From thence he was promoted to hold a menial office about the person of his great brother, into whose favour he at length rose by the murder, when only a boy of fourteen, of one of the *Vizier's* enemies. From that time his rise was steady, and as he rose so did he discard the follies and excesses of his youth, displaying a daring and heroic spirit, great military address, and a power of self-discipline and self-control unparalleled among the chiefs of Central Asia. To his hands was entrusted the execution of the *Vizier's* project for establishing the Barukzyes in Herat, then held by a brother of the reigning king.

The design was completely successful for the moment, owing to the daring and also to the treachery of Dost Mahomed, but the blow recoiled with fearful force on the person of the *Vizier*. Returning from his raid against the Persians, which had been the ostensible pretext for his march to Herat, Futteh Khan was seized by Prince Kamran, son of Mahmoud; his eyes were put out, and persisting in his refusal to give up his brother to the Prince's vengeance, he was hacked to pieces before the whole court.

This brutal act finally overthrew the long tottering dynasty of the Suddozyes, who had been kings in Cabul since Ahmed Shah founded the Afghan Empire in 1747. Dost Mahomed's vengeance was sudden and no less brutal. But it is impossible in this limited space to enter into all the details of his rise to the chief seat of power. It must suffice to say that when Lord Auckland entered on his government Dost Mahomed was firmly seated on the throne of Cabul, and the whole of the country in the hands of the Barukzye *Sirdars*, with the exception of Herat, where Kamran still reigned, the last remnant, save the exiled Soojah, of the legitimate line.

Shortly after Lord Auckland's arrival at Calcutta Dost Mahomed addressed to him a letter of congratulation on his assumption of office. Adverting to his quarrel with the Sikhs, who, under Runjeet Singh, the old one-eyed "Lion of the Punjab," had wrested the rich valley of Peshawur from the Afghan Empire, he said, " the late transactions in this quarter, the conduct of the reckless and misguided Sikhs, and their breach of treaty, are well known to your Lordship. Communicate to me whatever may suggest itself to your wisdom for the settlement of the affairs of this country, that it may serve as a rule for my guidance." And he concluded with a hope that "your Lordship will consider me and my country as your own."

To this complimentary effusion the Viceroy returned a suitable reply, assuring the *Ameer* of his wish that the Afghans should become a "flourishing and united nation," but declining to interfere in the Sikh quarrel, on the plea that it was not "the practice of the British Government to interfere with the affairs of other independent states." It was hinted, too, that "some gentleman" would probably be deputed to the *Ameer's* Court to discuss certain "commercial topics." This plan, which had originally commended itself to Lord William Bentinck, shortly after took effect in the despatch of Captain Alexander Burnes to Cabul.

But by this time affairs in Persia had reached a crisis. Though Mahomed Shah, breathing fire and sword against Herat, had ascended the throne in 1834, it was not till 1837 that his threats took practical shape. Despite the ceaseless promptings of the Russian minister at Teheran (who, it is perhaps needless to say, had, according to his own Government, done his best to dissuade Mahomed from any advance on the Afghan frontier), the *Shah* still hung back. If Kamran would send hostages and a large present, would own the Persian king as sovereign, coin money, and have prayers read in his name, all should be well.

The hostages and the present Kamran was content to allow, but the rest he could not stomach. The Barukzye chief who

16

ruled at Candahar viewed the proposed invasion with complaisance, hoping to secure Herat for himself, and being perfectly willing to hold it as a *fief* of Persia. He even went so far as to propose to send one of his sons to the Persian camp as hostage for his fidelity, and to secure the best terms for himself and his brothers. Dost Mahomed warned him that if he did so he would be made "to bite the finger of repentance," but the warning was disregarded.

Egged on by the flattering assurances of the inestimable advantages to be derived from a Persian alliance, that the Russian agent did not cease to lay before him, Kohun Dil Khan disobeyed the commands of his chief; the boy was to be sent, and the alliance was to be completed. Mahomed Shah then commenced his march against Herat, and at the same time Burnes appeared at Cabul. "Thus," says Kaye, "the seeds of the Afghan war were sown."

Burnes had been at Cabul before. He had gone there in 1832, with the sanction of Lord William Bentinck, and had been courteously received by Dost Mahomed, of whom he had formed a very favourable opinion, in contrast with that which he entertained of the weak and vacillating Soojah. His opinion of the *Ameer* was, probably, in the main a correct one, but he scarcely seems to have exercised his usual judgment when he declared the Afghans to be "a simple-minded, sober people, of frank and open manners." Returning in the following year, Burnes was sent to England to impart to the authorities at home the results of his travels and observations.

In London he was received with the greatest enthusiasm. His book was published, and read by everyone. He became the "lion" of the season, and the name of "Bokhara Burnes" was to be seen in every list of fashionable entertainments. Returning to India in 1835, he was soon removed from Cutch, where he had acted as Assistant to the Resident, on a mission to the *Ameers* of Sindh. While still engaged in that duty he received notice to hold himself in readiness to proceed to Cabul, and on November 26, 1836, he sailed from Bombay "to work out the policy of opening the River Indus to commerce." That Lord Auckland had at that time any idea, much less any definite plan, of interfering in Afghan politics is most unlikely, as it is certain Lord William Bentinck had not when he first thought of this "commercial" mission.

It is worthy of note, however, that when Burnes first broached the plan to the Court of Directors at home they refused to countenance it, feeling, in the words of the chairman, Mr. Tucker, "perfectly assured that it must soon degenerate into a political agency, and that we should, as a necessary consequence, be involved in all the entanglements of Afghan politics." Mr. Grant, of the Board of Control, held similar views, and Sir Charles Metcalfe in an emphatic minute pointed out the evils of this "commercial agency." The die, however, was cast, and on September 20, 1837, Burnes for the second time entered Cabul.

As before. Dost Mahomed received him with all courtesy, and with "great pomp and splendour." The navigation of the Indus soon disappeared into the background. From Burnes's own letters to Macnaghten, the Political Secretary at Calcutta, it may be seen how much of importance he himself attached to his commercial character. Nevertheless, at a private interview, "which lasted till midnight," with the *Ameer*, he talked a good deal about the Indus, and about trade, and other such harmless topics. The *Ameer* listened with the greatest attention, but when it came to his turn to speak, he substituted for the Indus the word Peshawur, and for commerce, the ability and resources of Runjeet Singh. If only he could regain Peshawur it was very evident that who so would might hold the trade of the Indus.

On this head Burnes was cautious. He suggested that possibly some arrangement might be concluded with Runjeet Singh by which Peshawur might be restored to the *Ameer's* brother Mahomed, from whose government the Sikhs had originally won it. But the *Ameer* wanted it for himself, and by no manner of means for his brother. Further than this, however, Burnes would not commit himself. He distinctly stated, moreover, that neither Dost Mahomed nor his brothers (should they decline the Persian alliance, of which the *Ameer*, and probably with sincerity, declared himself in no way desirous) must found any hopes on British aid. Sympathy he promised largely, should they behave themselves well, but not a single *rupee* nor a single musket. Still, even after this, the *Ameer* persisted in his professions of friendship to the English, nor is there any reason to doubt that he, at that time, meant what he said.

Nay, he even offered himself to compel his brothers at Candahar to break once and for all with the *Shah*; but this Burnes declined, exhorting him, however, to use all pacific means to influence them, and himself writing to Kohun Dil to threaten him with the displeasure of England if he continued his intrigues with the Persian and Russian Courts. At that particular time the Candahar chiefs had rather cooled in their desire for the Persian alliance, and began to have suspicions that instead of obtaining Herat they were not unlikely to lose Candahar. Burnes thereupon despatched Lieutenant Leech, an officer of his mission, to them, promising them that should the Persian army after the fall of Herat advance on Candahar, he would himself march with Dost Mahomed to their defence, which he would further with all the means in his power.

It was a bold step, but as many thought at the time, and as nearly all were agreed afterwards, it was by far the best that could have been taken. Lord Auckland, however, thought, or was advised to think otherwise. Burnes was severely censured for having so far exceeded his instructions—though he might well have pleaded in excuse that he knew not what were the instructions he had exceeded—and ordered at once to "set himself right with the chiefs." There was nothing left for him but to obey, and the result of his obedience was a treaty concluded between the chiefs and the *Shah* under a Russian guarantee.

Such a risk was not to be run again, nor was Burnes for the future to be able to plead any want of definite instructions. From this time forward his instructions were, indeed, explicit enough. Briefly they may be defined as to ask for everything and to give nothing. In vain did Dost Mahomed point out that in desiring to regain Peshawur from the Sikhs, he was doing practically no more than England was avowedly bent on doing, on guarding his frontier from danger, and that to exchange Runjeet Singh for his brother Mahomed was but to make his last state worse than his first. Burnes himself fully recognized the justice of his arguments, but Burnes's masters remained obstinately deaf.

All they would promise was to restrain Runjeet Singh from attacking Dost Mohamed, provided Dost Mohamed in return bound himself to abstain from an alliance with any other state. At this, says Burnes, the *Sirdars* only laughed. "Such a promise," said Jubbar Khan, the *Ameer's* brother, and a staunch champion of the English cause, "such a promise amounts to nothing, for we are not under the apprehension of any aggressions from Lahore; they have hitherto been on the side of the *Ameer*, not of Runjeet Singh, and yet for such a promise you expect us to desist from all intercourse with Russia, with Persia, with Toorkistan, with every nation but England."

To make matters still worse, at this crisis a new actor appeared on the scene, the Russian Vickovitch, bearing letters from Count Simonich and from the *Czar* himself, though the latter was unsigned, so as to be repudiated or acknowledged as events might require. The *Ameer*, still willing to please the British, offered to turn the Russian back from his gates, but that, Burnes pointed out, would be contrary to the rule of civilised nations, and Vickovitch was therefore allowed to enter Cabul and to present his letters, which were ostensibly, as those of Burnes had been, of a purely commercial bearing. What Burnes, however, thought of the arrival, he showed plainly enough in a letter written a few days after to a private friend.

"We are in a mess here," he writes. "The Emperor of Russia has sent an envoy to Cabul with a blazing letter three feet long, offering Dost Mahomed money to fight Runjeet Singh . . . . . It is now a neck-and-neck race between Russia and ourselves, and if his Lordship would hear reason he would forthwith send agents to Bokhara, Herat, Candahar, and Koondooz, not forgetting Sindh."

His Lordship, however, would not hear such reason as Burnes had to offer, and when on March 5th, 1838, certain specific demands were presented by the *Ameer*, that the English should protect Cabul and Candahar from Persia, that Runjeet Singh should he compelled to restore Peshawur, and various others of the same tendency, Burnes could only, in the name of the British Government, refuse his assent to any and all of them, and then sit down to write a formal request for his dismissal. One more attempt was made by Dost Mahomed to come to terms, but it was of no use.

The old ground was traversed again, and only with the old result. As a last resource the *Ameer* wrote to Lord Auckland in terms almost of humility, imploring him "to remedy the grievances of the Afghans," and to "give them a little encouragement and power." This was the last effort, and it failed. Then the game was up indeed. Vickovitch was sent for and received with every mark of honour; one of the Candahar chiefs came up in haste to Cabul, and on April 26th, 1838, Burnes turned his back on the Afghan capital.

As the Russian here disappears from our story a few words as to his subsequent career and end may not be out of place. After the departure of the English envoy he flung himself heart and soul into his business; promising men, promising money, promising everything that the *Ameer* asked. He even proposed to visit Lahore and use his good offices with Runjeet Singh, but that plea failed, owing chiefly to the address of Mackeson, our agent at Lahore. For a time the Russian was all-powerful throughout Afghanistan, but after the repulse of the Persians from Herat and the entry of the English into Cabul his star paled.

He proceeded to Teheran to give a full report of his doings to the Russian Minister there, and by him was ordered to proceed direct to St. Petersburg. Arrived there, flattered with hope, for he felt he had done all man could do, he reported himself to Count Nesselrode. The minister refused to see him. "I know no Captain Vickovitch," was the answer, "except an adventurer of that name who is reported to have been lately engaged in some un-

authorised intrigues at Cabul and Candahar."Vickovitch under-
stood the answer thoroughly. He knew that severe remonstrance
had been sent from London to St. Petersburg; he knew his own
Government only too well. He went home, burnt his papers,
wrote a few lines of reproach, and blew his brains out.

To return to Cabul. Notwithstanding the Russian promises,
and the exultation of his brothers at Candahar, the *Ameer* felt
that he had acted unwisely.Very soon he saw that Russia could
do little more than promise, and that England had made up her
mind to perform. Despite Russian money and Russian men, the
Shah could not force his way into Herat while Eldred Pottinger
stood behind the crumbling walls, and a vast army was assem-
bling on the banks of the Indus to drive Dost Mahomed and the
whole Barukzye clan from power.

To keep friends with the Afghan ruler and to preserve the
independence of his Empire was the obvious policy of the British Government. But the authorities at Simlah, Lord Auckland,
Mr. Macnaghten, Mr. Henry Torrens and Mr. John Colvin, had
determined that that ruler should be, not the Barukzye Dost
Mahomed, a man of proved energy and ability, who had shown
himself anxious to cultivate the friendship of England, and who
possessed the confidence and the favour of his subjects, but the
Suddozye Shah Soojah, who, though born of the legitimate line,
was no less a usurper than Dost Mahomed himself, who was
regarded by the majority of his countrymen with indifference
and contempt, and who more than once had proved alike his
inability to administer and to maintain dominion.

By what process of reasoning the Viceroy arrived at this remarkable conclusion has never been made perfectly clear, but
though he alone, notwithstanding Sir John Hobhouse's gener-
ous declaration from the Board of Control, will be, rightly or
wrongly, held by posterity responsible for the disastrous events
which followed, it is at least to his credit that he left no stone
unturned to arrive at the opinions of all competent advisers
before deciding on his own. Prominent among these was Mr.
McNeill, then our envoy at the Court of Teheran, a man of keen

powers of observation and undoubted ability, who may be said to share with Pottinger the glory of the Persian repulse from Herat. His plan, as he impressed more than once on Burnes, was to consolidate the Afghan Empire under Dost Mahomed.

Placing no reliance on the sincerity of the Candahar chiefs, he yet entertained a high opinion of the *Ameer* himself, whom he would have been well pleased to see established in Herat and Candahar as well as in Cabul. McNeill's correspondence, however, had to pass through the hands of Captain, afterwards Sir Claudius, Wade, himself also well versed in the politics of Central Asia, and at that time holding the responsible post of Governor-General's Agent on the North-Western Frontier.

Wade forwarded a copy of McNeill's letter to the Governor, and forwarded with it one from himself in which he strongly deprecated the policy of consolidation. To him it seemed better that the Afghan Empire should remain, as it then was, subdivided into practically independent states, each of whom, as he conceived, would be more likely in their own interests to court our friendship and to meet our views, than if brought under the yoke of one ruler, to whom they could never be expected to yield a passive obedience.

"Supposing," he continued, "we were to aid Dost Mahomed to overthrow in the first place his brother at Candahar, and then his Suddozye rival at Herat, what would be the consequence? As the system of which it is intended to be a part would go to gratify the longing wish of Mahomed Shah for the annexation of Herat to his dominions, the first results would be that the Shah-Zadah Kamran would apply to Persia, and offer, on the condition of her assistance to save him from the fate which impended over his head, to submit to all the demands of that General, which Kamran has hitherto so resolutely and successfully resisted, and between his fears and the attempts of Dost Mahomed to take it, Herat, which is regarded by everyone who has studied its situation as the key to Afghanistan, would inevitably fall prostrate before the arms of Persia, by the effect of the very measures which we had designed for its security from

Persian thraldom."

That it was our interest to maintain the independence of Herat was obvious, so long as Herat was able to remain in the position it was then assuming, that of a barrier against Russo-Persian invasion. Prince Kamran was, in fact, then playing our game as well as we could have played it ourselves. But the question was, how long would Herat be able to retain its independence? The fall of Herat meant the fall of Candahar, and the absorption of all Southern and Western Afghanistan into a Persian province, and a Persian province was then but another name for a Russian province. Could it have been possible, and that McNeill thought it possible was a strong argument in its favour, to consolidate the various states under one ruler strong enough to retain the reins when once placed in his hands, Herat and Candahar would have been secured forever, and there would have arisen in a united Afghanistan a perpetual barrier to Russian ambition.

Had we come to terms with Dost Mahomed, in all human probability we should not have had to chastise the insolence of his son. Burnes for his part still championed the cause of the *Ameer*, urging that it was not yet too late to secure his friendship, that, despite all that had taken place, he still wanted only the smallest encouragement to range himself on our side, and that as whatever action was taken could not be taken save at some cost, the money could not be better spent than on Dost Mahomed. But when Burnes's opinion was asked, the Government had already decided on their policy, and as Dost Mahomed was to go, he was only asked to pronounce on the expediency of choosing Soojah as his successor.

It seemed to him that McNeill's plan, of which he was a staunch advocate, would be better served by restoring Soojah to his crown than by giving it to Sultan Mahomed or any other of the chiefs, who would probably be but a tool in the hands of the Sikhs, themselves objects of bitter hatred to the Afghans. As the Government, then, were committed to one of two evils, Burnes gave his vote in favour of that which seemed to him the least, and which he, in common with the rest of the Council, believed could be accomplished with little danger and at comparatively little expense.

Lord Auckland's first idea was that the deposition of Dost Mahomed should be effected by the combined forces of Runjeet Singh and Soojah, raised and drilled under British supervision, and assisted by British gold—in Kaye's words, "England was to remain in the background, jingling the money-bag." Such were the first instructions issued to the Mission sent in May, 1838, to sound Runjeet Singh on the design, but scarcely had they been written when the thought of employing British troops seems first to have dawned in, or been introduced into Lord Auckland's mind. He would have preferred that the two Princes should undertake the work on their own account, while he contributed merely his countenance and perhaps some money, but he was very doubtful whether the Princes would see the matter in the same light.

Macnaghten, the leader of the mission, was instructed therefore to suggest the first course to Runjeet Singh, and should he view that with disfavour, to hold out the possibility of some sort of "demonstration" being undertaken by British troops from some convenient point. The event proved that Lord Auckland's doubts were just. The Sikh Prince heard the proposal for restoring Soojah with pleasure, and at once gave his consent to the plan; but when Macnaghten, cautiously feeling his way, hinted that an army of Sikhs, together with such a force as Soojah could raise with British help, would be amply sufficient, the crafty old man stopped him with an emphatic refusal.

That England should become a third party to the treaty already existing between him and Soojah was, in his own phrase "adding sugar to milk;" he was willing, moreover, himself to play such a part as England might deem necessary; but with the independent expedition he would have nothing to do. Macnaghten therefore at once returned to his original proposal, and after a good deal of fencing and delay on Runjeet Singh's part, the treaty was concluded. From Soojah, of course, little difficulty was to be anticipated, but he, unlike Runjeet Singh, though willing to employ British gold and British skill in equipping and disciplining the forces he declared his ability at once to bring to his standard, was by no means anxious to see a British force in the field with him.

He was doubtful what effect such an apparition in their strongholds might have upon his countrymen, nor was he at all desirous to appear as owing his throne to British bayonets. He proposed that his own force should proceed by way of the Bolan Pass on Candahar and Ghuznee, while the Sikhs, with whom should go his son Timour, should march on the capital through the Khyber and Koord-Cabul defiles. Already, he said, had he received offers of allegiance from numerous chiefs discontented with the Barukzye rule, and offended at Dost Mahomed's alliance with the Persians, prominent among whom appeared, strangely enough, the name of Abdoolah Khan, destined to become the prime mover in the insurrection which ultimately cost Soojah his life, and restored the Barukzye dynasty.

"The faggots," they wrote, "are ready; it only requires the lighted torch to be applied." Soojah therefore was urgent with Macnaghten that he should be allowed to accomplish his restoration with his own troops, as he expressed himself confident of doing; a feat which would greatly tend to raise his character among his countrymen, while the fact of his being "upheld by foreign force alone could not fail to detract in a great measure from his dignity and consequence." Soojah's wishes, in fact, tallied precisely with Lord Auckland's original design, but every day brought fresh complications, with fresh confirmation of the impracticability of that design.

First Soojah and Runjeet Singh alone were to be the agents; then a British force was to "demonstrate" in reserve at Shikarpoor; next a few British regiments were to be added to Soojah's levies. Finally, all these plans were dismissed, and one wholly different to any Lord Auckland had hitherto dreamed of was substituted in their stead.

Sir Henry Fane, commander-in-chief of the British army in India, was then at Simlah, with Lord Auckland. That he had from the first disapproved of English interference with Afghan politics the following passage from his correspondence with Sir Charles Metcalfe, written in 1837, sufficiently proves.

> Every advance you might make beyond the Sutlej to the westward, in my opinion, adds to your military weakness . . . . if you want your empire to expand, expand it over Oude or over Gwalior and the remains of the Mahratta Empire. Make yourselves complete sovereigns of all within your bounds, *but let alone the far West.*

But as it had been decided that the work was to be done, he was vehement in his opinion that it should be done as thoroughly as possible. With a "fine old Tory" contempt of anything approaching to economy, he advised the employment of a regular British force, horse, foot, and artillery, with which there could be no possibility of a reverse, a contingency in the peculiar circumstances of the case to be guarded against with more than common care. There were, still nearer to the Viceroy's person, other and even warmer advocates of the same policy; so after some weeks of suspense and oscillation Lord Auckland yielded, and the fiat for the "Army of the Indus" went forth.

In August the regiments selected were warned for field service, and in September a General Order published the constitution of the force. It was to be divided into two columns, the Bengal column and the Bombay column. The former was to consist of a brigade of artillery under Colonel Graham; a brigade of cavalry under Colonel Arnold; and five brigades of infantry under Colonels Sale and Dennie, of Her Majesty's, and Colonels Nott, Roberts, and Worseley, of the Company's service. The latter were told off into two divisions under Sir Willoughby Cotton, an officer of Her Majesty's army, who had seen service in the Burmese war, and Major-General Duncan, of the Company's army.

The whole was to be under the personal command of Sir Henry Fane himself. The Bombay column was to consist of a brigade of artillery under Colonel Stevenson; a brigade of cavalry under Major-General Thackwell; a brigade of infantry under Major-General Wiltshire; the whole to be under the command of Sir John Keane, commander-in-chief of the Bombay army. The English regiments selected were, besides the artillery, in the Bengal column, the 16th Lancers and the 3rd and 13th Regiments of the Line; in the Bombay column, the 4th Dragoons and the 2nd and 17th Regiments of the Line.

Besides these troops, Soojah's own levies were being actively raised on the other side of the Indus, under the supervision of Captain Wade, who found it no easy matter to quiet the Afghan's not unfounded fears lest he should come to be no more than a puppet in the hands of the English officers, and his restoration finally effected, not by his own arms, but by the English bayonets. Though the sympathies of the majority of our army were rather with Dost Mahomed than with Soojah, and it was far from clear to them on what pretext they were to invade the former's kingdom, the prospect of active employment after so many years of repose was popular with all classes of military men, and from every quarter of India officers, leaving without a murmur the luxurious ease of well-paid staff appointments, made haste to rejoin their regiments.

Scarcely less important than the selection of the military commands was the selection of the envoys who were to accompany the different columns in a political capacity. Wade of course was to march with the Sikh force destined to escort Prince Timour through the Khyber Pass to his father's capital, but it was not so easy to determine on whom should devolve the delicate duty of directing the mind of Soojah himself, and shaping the political course of his operations. Sir Henry Fane not unreasonably wished that the entire control, political as well as military, should be vested in his own hands, and proposed to take Burnes with him as his confidential adviser.

But Lord Auckland had other views, and, contrary to general expectation, his choice fell on Macnaghten, under whom Burnes, after a momentary, and not unnatural, fit of disgust, agreed to serve in a subordinate capacity, believing, in common with others, that Soojah once firmly seated on the throne, Macnaghten would return, and the chief control of affairs would then devolve upon him.

On October 1st the Declaration of War was issued. If our officers were doubtful before as to the right of their cause this document certainly tended but little to solve their doubts. Hardly, moreover, had the Simlah manifesto had time to penetrate through India when news arrived of the raising of the siege of Herat. As the deliverance of Herat, and Western Afghanistan generally, from Persian rule had formed, according to the proclamation, the principal object of the expedition, it was supposed that the English army would now be disbanded, and Soojah and Runjeet Singh left to their own devices. Even those of the authorities at home who had allowed that while a Persian force was still at the gates of Herat Lord Auckland could not do otherwise than prepare for its defence, were unanimously of opinion that the motive for the expedition had now ceased to exist.

Among such authorities conspicuously appear the names of the Duke of Wellington, Lord Wellesley, Sir Charles Metcalfe, Mountstuart Elphinstone, and others of scarce less weight and experience. Lord Auckland and his advisers were not, however, of this number. The army was to be reduced in strength, it is true, since there was no longer any prospect of an encounter with Persia, or possibly with Russia, but the expedition was in no way to be abandoned. Instead of two divisions the Bengal column was to consist only of one; two brigades of infantry were to be left behind; and the cavalry and artillery were to be proportionately reduced.

Nor was Sir Henry Fane inclined to retain the command of a force whose numbers were so diminished, and whose probabilities of action were so limited. The Bengal column was therefore placed in the hands of Sir Willoughby Cotton, and on its junction with the column from Bombay the chief command was to fall to Sir John Keane, who led the latter force.

All things were now ready, but before the army broke ground a grand ceremony was to take place, a ceremony which had indeed been arranged before any note of war had been sounded. On November 29th Lord Auckland and Runjeet Singh met at Ferozepore. It was a magnificent pageant. The Viceroy's camp was pitched about four miles from the River Gharra. The English army lay on the plain, a noble force, in perfect order and condition, and brought together, according to Havelock, in a manner that had never before been equalled.

Escorted by the principal military and political English officers, Runjeet Singh rode up on his elephant through a splendid guard of honour, amid the thunder of artillery and the clash of innumerable bands, to the *Durbar* tent. Lord Auckland and Sir Henry Fane rode out to meet him, and as the two cavalcades joined such was the crush and uproar that many of the Sikh chiefs, thinking there was some design afoot on their prince, began "to blow their matches and grasp their weapons with a mingled air of distrust and ferocity."

With some difficulty a passage was cleared, and the little decrepit old man, supported by the Viceroy and the commander-in-chief, entered the tent where the costly presents prepared for him were laid out. Ordnance of British make, horses and elephants magnificently caparisoned, were all inspected and admired, and, while a royal salute thundered without, the prince bowed low before a picture of Queen Victoria, borne into his presence by Sir Willoughby Cotton. As the infirm old chief was being conducted round the tent he stumbled and fell to the ground at the very muzzle of one of the British guns.

A murmur of horror arose from his *Sirdars* at so dire an omen, but as the Viceroy and Sir Henry Fane hastened to raise him to his feet, their hearts were comforted by the reflection that though their chief had fallen before the British guns, the highest representatives of the British Queen had raised him again to his feet.

On the following day the visit was returned amid a scene of still greater splendour and variety. According to an eyewitness "the Sikhs shone down the English." All the great *Sirdars* were present in their most gorgeous trappings and mounted on their finest steeds, while from a Sikh band the strains of our own national anthem rose upon the air, and from the Sikh guns pealed forth the salute ordained for royalty alone. It must be confessed, however, that Runjeet Singh's ideas of ceremony were not all of the same exalted nature. At a later period of the day, after all the due formalities were over, the Viceroy was required to be present at "an unseemly display of dancing girls, and the antics of some male buffoons."

The two following days were devoted to military exercises. On the first Sir Henry Fane manoeuvred the British force with elaborate skill and display; and on the second the Sikh cavalry executed some less intricate movements with the unqualified approval of their experienced critics.

With this the ceremony was at an end. Runjeet Singh returned to Lahore, and the Viceroy followed him on his first visit to the Sikh principality. The final dispositions and selections were made by the commander-in-chief. A few weeks previously Soojah's levies, about 6000 strong, horse, foot, and artillery, under the command of Major-General Simpson, had left Loodhianah on their way to the front, and on December 10th, 1838, the British troops marched out from Ferozepore on their first stage to the Afghan capital.

A glance at the map will suffice to show that a more direct route might have been found from Ferozepore to Cabul than down the bank of the Indus to Bukkur, thence, across the river, by Shikarpoor and Dadur, through the Bolan Pass, to Quettah, and from Quettah, through the Kojuck, by Candahar and Ghuznee to Cabul. In short, as Kaye points out, the army was about to traverse two sides of a triangle, instead of shaping its course along a third. But there were two important reasons for the choice of the longer route. In the first place, Runjeet Singh had strong objections to opening the Punjab to our troops; and in the second place the *Ameers* of Sindh were to be "coerced."

Shikarpoor, on the northern bank of the Indus, had originally formed a part of the great Douranee Empire, handed down by Timour to Zemaun Shah and his brothers, intact as it had been received from the founder, Ahmed. But piece by piece the kingdom had been dismembered through the quarrels and weaknesses of its rulers. Cashmere, and Mooltan, and Peshawur had been won by the Sikhs; Herat had risen to independence; while Shikarpoor with a fair slice of the southern frontier had passed to the Ameers of Sindh.

But though Shikarpoor was theirs, they held, or had held it, in consideration only of a yearly tribute, which tribute, unpaid through many years, had now swelled, as Soojah maintained, to no less a sum than twenty *lakhs* of *rupees*, a sum gratuitously increased by the English Government to twenty-five *lakhs*, that the terms of Runjeet Singh (who was to have received half, but had lately increased his wants) might be granted without Soojah being the sufferer. The *Ameers* themselves, however, told a different tale. Independently of their not unreasonable objections to the validity of a claim that had been suffered to slumber for upwards of thirty years, they were enabled triumphantly, as they supposed, to point to two releases of the debt, written in Korans, and signed and sealed by Soojah.

Thus fortified, they declared to Colonel Pottinger, our agent at Hyderabad, that "they were sure the Governor-General did not intend to make them pay again for what they had already bought and obtained, in the most binding way, a receipt in full"—a mark of confidence which Pottinger was instructed to demolish without delay. Nor was this the only difficulty that the passage through Sindh promised to present. In the treaty which had opened the Indus to navigation, it had been expressly stipulated that the river should be free to commerce only, and it became therefore necessary, for the transport of our army, that this treaty should be broken.

Pottinger, sorely against his will, was ordered to point out to the *Ameers* that if they placed any obstacles in the way of the "first and necessary" undertaking on which their English friends had embarked, it would be the painful duty of those friends to take steps to ensure a more ready and hearty co-operation. In other words, the *Ameers* were told that if they did not do what

32

was wanted of them, they would be turned out to make room for those who would. They must pay the twenty-five *lakhs* of *rupees*, the greater part of which would go into the pockets of a man to whom they were indebted not one single *anna*; they must consent to the violation of the treaty of the Indus, and they must further the advance of our army through their territory in every possible way. If they did not agree to these demands, they would find the consequences disagreeable.

It did not at first appear that they were likely to agree. Burnes had, indeed, managed to settle the difficulty of the Indus, and the *Ameers* of Khyrpore, more tractable than the Hyderabad princes, had agreed temporarily to cede to the British the fortress of Bukkur, the point selected for the passage. Soojah with his levies, who were some days' march in advance of the Bengal column, had already crossed, and was waiting our arrival at Shikarpoor, but for a while it seemed extremely doubtful when we should be able to join him.

The *Ameers* were waxing turbulent. They had grossly insulted Pottinger, and were openly collecting forces for the defence of their capital. It was feared that the "painful duty" would be found necessary, and orders were despatched to Keane (who had landed with the Bombay army at Vikkur in the end of November, but had been temporarily delayed at Tattah for want of carriage) to prepare to co-operate with Cotton against Hyderabad. As the Bombay column moved up the right bank of the river, the Bengal column, against the urgent remonstrances of Macnaghten, moved down the left bank to meet it. Both forces were in the highest spirits.

The defences of Hyderabad were known to be weak; its treasures were believed to be immense, and a prospect of unbounded loot danced before the eyes of a soldiery who had almost forgotten what the word meant. At the eleventh hour, however, the enchanting prospect faded. The *Ameers* consented to our demands; a part of the tribute was paid, and Hyderabad was saved for a time; while, what was then of still more importance, a collision between the military and political authorities was avoided.

On February 20th, 1839, Cotton was at Shikarpoor, and again differences between him and Macnaghten seemed imminent. Soojah had found himself short of carriage, and Macnaghten had asked Cotton to supply him with 1000 camels from his own train. But the General expressed himself strongly to the effect that if Soojah was unable to advance his men, it were far better that Soojah and his men should be left behind than that their wants should be relieved at the expense of the English troops. It was but too apparent, even at that early stage, that the English military officers were inclined to look upon Soojah and his 6000 soldiers as altogether superfluous. He was, indeed, a king who was to be restored to his throne, but until the throne was ready for him it would be better for all parties that he should remain in the background.

Macnaghten, keenly alive to the danger of such sentiments, and feeling himself especially bound, both in honour and interest, to uphold the cause of our ally, combated the military policy resolutely. A collision was happily averted by the timely arrival of despatches from the Viceroy, strongly tending to confirm Macnaghten's views; nevertheless, when the English force advanced, three days afterwards, the carriage difficulty had not been solved, and Soojah with his levies remained at Shikarpoor. Keane, who came up with the Bombay army some days later, though little less willing, was more able to help; but the king, who had fondly hoped to head the advance into his own kingdom, was, for the time, compelled to content himself with a second place.

Cotton's march through the Bolan Pass to Quettah, though arduous and painful, was unopposed. Many of the camels and other beasts of burden dropped dead on the route from want of water; there was considerable desertion among the camp followers, and some plundering on the part of the Beloochees, but progress was steadily made, and on March 26th the column reached Quettah, "a most miserable mud town, with a small castle on a mound, on which there was a small gun on a rickety carriage."

Here there seemed a fair prospect of sheer starvation. Stores, as well as baggage, had been abandoned among the rugged defiles of the Bolan Pass, and Mehrab Khan, the Beloochee Prince of Khelat, with whom Burnes had concluded a treaty in our favour, either could not, or would not, help. He declared that there was very little grain in his country, and Burnes could not prove that he did not speak truth, while he was bound to allow the *Khan's* plea that much of the alleged scarcity was owing, though unavoidably owing, to our own presence. He could not, therefore, conscientiously recommend Macnaghten to sanction Cotton's proposal for a movement on Khelat, though convinced in his own mind of our ally's treachery, and when Keane, arriving at Quettah on April 6th, assumed the chief command, it was decided to push on for Candahar with all possible speed.

Save for the heat, and the scarcity of water, the advance proceeded uneventfully enough. Our soldiers behaved admirably under circumstances peculiarly trying to Europeans, and experienced by many of them for the first time. George Lawrence (one of the three owners of a name which is a household word throughout India, at that time a captain of the 2nd Bengal Light Cavalry) relates how he saw a trooper of the 16th Lancers pour the contents of a soda-water bottle half full of water, a treasure then worth its weight in gold, down the throat of a native child on the point of perishing from thirst.

As the army neared Candahar Soojah was moved up again to the front, and many of the chiefs and people of Western Afghanistan hastened to his standard. It was known that Kohun Dil Khan had fled, that there was open dissension among the Barukzye brotherhood, and it soon became clear that if a stand was to be made it would be made at a point nearer Cabul. On April 25th, Shah Soojah-ool-Moolk, after more than thirty years of exile, re-entered in bloodless triumph the southern capital of his kingdom.

Till June 27th the army lay at Candahar, waiting the ripening of the crops. So long a period of forced inactivity was distasteful to the troops, while daily the conviction forced itself on the more observant of the officers that the popularity which Soojah had claimed for himself existed only in his own imagination. The Douranee tribes had, indeed, long yearned to shake off the hateful yoke of the Barukzye *Sirdars*, by whom they had been systematically plundered and oppressed; but they lacked both spirit and strength to make common cause with their promised deliverer, while both their national and religious feelings were alike stirred by the appearance within their gates of the accursed infidels.

When the first cravings of curiosity had been gratified, their attitude to their king was one rather of indifference than devotion, and to us one of undisguised if not active enmity. It needed not the warning of Soojah to remind the English that they were no longer in Hindostan. Two young officers, Inverarity, of the 16th Lancers, and Wilmer, were attacked at a short distance from camp; Inverarity was murdered, and his companion escaped with difficulty. The Ghilzyes, a fierce and lawless tribe, the original lords of the soil, alike rejecting British gold and British promises, began, too, to give early promise of the stern opposition that was hereafter to be experienced from them.

When, a fortnight after his arrival, Soojah held a grand state reception, scarcely one of his subjects appeared to do homage to their king. A royal salute of 101 guns was fired in his honour; the British troops marched past his throne in imposing array, and Soojah, highly elated, declared that the moral influence of the ceremony would be felt "from Pekin to Constantinople." But in reality, the whole affair, so far as what should have been its most important features were concerned, was a miserable failure. Lawrence relates a significant speech made to him by an Afghan of distinction, whom he fell in with while on reconnoitring service to the front.

"What could induce you," said the man, "to squander *crores* of *rupees* in coming to a poor rocky country like ours, without wood or water, in order to force upon us an unlucky person as a king, who, the moment you turn your backs, will be upset by Dost Mahomed, our own king?"

The order to advance given on June 27th was heard therefore with pleasure by all; and on July 21st the army was encamped before the famous citadel of Ghuznee.

It became soon evident that a serious mistake had been committed. Ghuznee was deservedly considered the strongest fortress in the country, and its defences were the boast of all Afghanistan. Keane had, indeed, been advised to the contrary, but he knew at least that it was garrisoned by about 3000 of the enemy under Hyder Khan, one of the *Ameer's* sons, while another was reported to be in the neighbourhood with a strong body of horse. Nevertheless, discarding the battering train, which had been tugged up to Candahar with immense labour and expense, he resumed his march with light field-pieces only, and found himself accordingly before a place subsequently described by himself as one "of great strength, both by nature and art," without the means of effecting a breach in its walls.

Our light companies soon cleared the villages and gardens surrounding the fort, not, however, without some loss, and at daybreak on the 22nd Keane and Cotton, with a party of engineers, reconnoitred the place from the heights commanding the eastern face. It was perfectly evident that the field-pieces might for all practical purposes have been left behind with the siege train at Candahar, but treachery was to show us a way in, which we could have found for ourselves only at immense loss.

One of the garrison, a Barukzye of rank, nephew to the *Ameer* himself, had deserted to our camp; the gates, he assured us, had all been built up with the exception of the Cabul gate, and by the Cabul gate therefore it was decided that the entrance should be made. That very night was chosen for the attack. Four English regiments were detailed for service; the 2nd, 13th, and 17th of the Line, and the Company's European Regiment. Colonel Dennie, of the 13th, was to lead the advance, consisting of the light companies of the four regiments, and the main column was placed under Brigadier Sale.

Captain Thomson, of the Bengal Engineers, was to superintend the explosion party, with his two subalterns, Durand (afterwards Sir Henry Durand) and Macleod, and Captain Peat, of the Bombay corps. The night was dark and stormy. The light guns were ordered to open fire, to distract the attention of the garrison, while the powder-bags were piled at the gate. The work was done quickly, quietly and well. Durand, according to one account, finding the first application of the port-fire of no effect, was obliged to scrape the hose with his finger-nails; then the powder exploded, and with a mighty crash, heard above the roaring of the guns and the noise of the storm, down, amid a column of black smoke, came huge masses of timber and masonry in dire confusion.

In rushed Dennie at the head of the stormers, and after him pressed Sale with the main column. The resistance, though short, was stubborn. The breach was still so narrow that entrance was difficult and slow. Dennie had won his way inside, but between him and Sale a strong party of the garrison had made their way to the gate. The Brigadier himself was cut down, but after a desperate struggle regained his feet, cleaving his opponent to the chin.

The supports, under Colonel Croker, pushed forward manfully, and as the day broke the colours of the 13th and 17th Regiments were flung out to the morning breeze on the ramparts of the Afghans' strongest fort. Ghuznee was ours, with a loss of 17 killed and 165 wounded, of whom 18 were officers. The loss of the garrison was never accurately known. Upwards of 500 were buried by our men, and many more were supposed to have fallen beyond the walls under the sabres of our cavalry; 1600 prisoners were taken, and large stores of grain and flour proved a welcome addition to the value of the prize.

With the fall of Ghuznee fell the hopes of Dost Mahomed. Within little more than twenty-four hours the news had reached him, and his brother, Jubbar Khan, was forthwith despatched to the English camp, proffering submission to Soojah, but claiming for his brother the office of *Vizier*, which had come to be considered a sort of hereditary appanage of the Barukzye clan. The offer was declined, and what Kaye calls the "mockery" of an honourable asylum in the British dominions suggested in its stead. With an indignant refusal the envoy returned to his brother, and Dost Mahomed then resolved on one last attempt. He moved out from the capital, designing to take up his ground at Maidan, a well-chosen spot on the Cabul River.

But when he had reached Urgundeh, he saw too clearly that the game was up. Hadji Khan, a man in whom he had placed peculiar reliance, had gone over to the enemy; the Kuzzilbashes were leaving him fast. With the *Koran* in his hand, he rode among his troops. "You have eaten my salt," he said, "these thirteen years. If, as is too plain, you are resolved to seek a new master, grant me but one favour in requital for that long period of maintenance and kindness—enable me to die with honour. Stand by the brother of Futteh Khan while he executes one last charge against the cavalry of these *Feringhee* dogs; in that onset he will fall; then go and make you own terms with Shah Soojah."

The appeal was in vain. Dismissing all of his followers who were minded to purchase safety by bowing to the new allegiance, he turned his horse's head, and rode towards the Hindoo-Koosh. A party of horse under the gallant Outram was despatched in hot pursuit. Twelve English officers rode with him, Lawrence among the number, and about 200 of our own men. Had the party been no larger it is probable that it would not have been left to Dost Mahomed to surrender at his own discretion. But in an evil hour it was decided that Hadji Khan with 500 Afghans should be added, and the dilatoriness of our "allies" wholly neutralised the energies of our own men.

Hadji, a traitor once, remained a traitor still, and though quick to leave his master in the hour of his misfortunes, he had no intention, with an eye to future contingencies, to commit himself beyond hope of recall. The harder, then, Outram and his troops rode, the slower rode the *Khan* and his following; every pretext that the ingenious Eastern mind could devise for delay was turned to account, and as the country was wholly unknown to the English leader he could not leave Hadji to his devices and push on alone after the fugitive. His orders were not to continue the chase beyond the Afghan frontier.

On August 9th he reached Bamean, to find that his game was but a day's march before him; but that one day's march had sounded the recall. Dost Mahomed was over the frontier, and there was nothing left for Outram but to return, to be laughed at for his "wild-goose chase," and to hear from the commander-in-chief that " he had not supposed there were thirteen such asses in his whole force!" It is satisfactory, however, to know that the traitor Hadji had this time over-reached himself. Outram reported his conduct on his return; other proofs of his treason were forthcoming; he was arrested by order of the king, and spent the remainder of his life a state prisoner in Hindostan.

So Soojah was once more seated on the throne of Cabul. He had entered the city on August 6th in royal pomp, resplendent with jewels (among which the mighty Koh-i-noor was this time conspicuous by its absence), mounted on a white charger, half smothered in golden trappings; Macnaghten and Burnes, in diplomatic costume, rode with him, and all the chief officers of the English army swelled his train.

But there was no popular enthusiasm; there were no loyal cries of welcome. The people flocked to stare at the show, but it was at the white-faced strangers they stared, not at their restored king. Still, the work had been done. The English flag had waved over Candahar and Ghuznee; an English army was encamped before Cabul. The usurpers were in flight, and the "rightful" king had returned again to his own.

According to the original terms of the proclamation, the British troops, their mission accomplished, were at once to withdraw from the country. Soojah himself was anxious to be rid of allies in whose hands he was conscious he was and could be no more than a puppet, and whose presence m the kingdom was a standing testimony to the absence of that loyalty which he had so loudly vaunted. Nothing would have better pleased the English themselves than to have acquiesced in the king's wishes; nothing would have pleased Lord Auckland better than that they should do so.

But it could not be. Unprotected by British bayonets the throne of the new king would not have stood for a day, and with it would have fallen the feeble fabric on which the "justice" of the expedition rested. The Simlah manifesto had declared that Soojah's "popularity throughout Afghanistan had been proved to his lordship by the strong and unanimous testimony of the best authorities;" how then could his lordship leave Soojah alone to give the lie to his own manifesto? But though it was expedient that an English force should still, at least for a time, continue at the king's right hand, it was neither expedient, nor, as it was thought, necessary that the entire army should remain.

A garrison at Cabul and Candahar, and others at the principal posts on the main roads to Hindostan, Ghuznee and Quettah on the west, and Jellalabad and Ali-Musjid on the east, would be amply sufficient. These could be furnished by a portion of the Bengal army, and the remainder could be withdrawn by way of Jellalabad and the Khyber Pass, while the Bombay column could return *en masse* through the Bolan Pass. Such was the advice of the commander-in-chief, and such, as it soon appeared, was the opinion of the Viceroy himself.

Before, however, the homeward march began Wade had brought Prince Timour to his father's court. Wade's share in the expedition, though dwarfed by the more brilliant exploits of Keane, had, notwithstanding the disaffection of the Sikhs (who, after Runjeet Singh's death, had not cared to conceal their dislike of their English allies), been performed with complete success, and had moreover materially assisted the march of the larger force.

For a long time Dost Mahomed had regarded the advance through the Khyber with far greater anxiety than that along the Western route, and though his troops had never actually encountered Wade in the field, a considerable detachment had been withdrawn for that purpose from the main army at a very critical moment. The official order for the departure of the troops appeared on October 2nd. It was at once seen that the first plan had been considerably altered. Nearly the whole of the Bengal division was to remain behind under Cotton, and only a comparatively small detachment was to return home with Keane and the Bombay army. Though Dost Mahomed had fled the kingdom, he was known to be still near at hand, a guest among the fiery and hostile Oosbegs, with whom he might at any rate seriously harass the frontier, if not, indeed, find himself strong enough to hazard an advance upon the capital.

A detachment had therefore been sent up in September to the Hindoo-Koosh, and it became necessary to supply their place at Cabul. The 13th, 40th, and 41st were the English regiments that remained. Of these, the first named, with the 35th Bengal Native Infantry and three light field guns, was stationed at Cabul, under Dennie. Jellalabad was garrisoned by the 48th Bengal Native Infantry, the 3rd Bengal Light Cavalry, some Sappers and Miners, three light guns, and a detachment of Skinner's Horse.

At Candahar, under Nott, were the 40th and 41st Regiments of the Line, the 42nd and 43rd Regiments of Bengal Native Infantry, a company of the European Bengal Artillery, two regiments of Soojah's Irregular Infantry, one of his Cavalry, and a troop of his Horse Artillery. MacLaren held Ghuznee with the 16th Bengal Native Infantry, some of Skinner's Horse, and certain details of Soojah's levies. At Quettah was a small force composed of Soojah's troops only, while the Kojuck Pass was watched by a body of Afghan horse, under Bosanquet, of the Bengal Infantry. At each of these posts was also stationed a political officer.

Shortly after the departure of Keane with the homeward-bound column, Soojah left the cold of the capital for the milder air of Jellalabad, and with him went Macnaghten, leaving Burnes in charge at Cabul. The winter months were passed in comparative quiet. Macnaghten busied himself with an attempt to win the favour of the turbulent Khyber tribes, and by lavish payments did succeed in lulling them to temporary quiet. There, too, was received news of the fall of Khelat, which had been determined on during the upward march as punishment for Mehrab Khan's treachery, and still more important news from the Bamean of the further flight of Dost Mohamed to the court of the Ameer of Bokhara, where our own envoy Stoddart was then a close prisoner in imminent danger of death.

But as a set-off against so much that was good to hear there came from Burnes the disquieting intelligence of the advance of a large Russian force from Orenberg on Khiva, ostensibly to release certain Russian merchants from captivity, and to punish the Khan, not too severely, for general misconduct—a pretext which, it will probably be remembered, was used with great effect on a subsequent occasion. Macnaghten was inclined at first to make light of the news, on which Burnes had, on the contrary, laid the greatest stress; but as rumour grew he consented at last to despatch a mission to the Russian camp.

Conolly and Rawlinson were selected—Burnes, when the post was offered to him, having only replied "that he would willingly go if he was ordered" —when, on the eve of their departure, the welcome news arrived that there was no longer a Russian camp for them to visit. Snow, pestilence and famine had done the work that neither Tartar sabres nor English diplomacy would have probably availed to do then, any more than they have availed since, and of Peroffski's 6000 men scarcely a man found his way back to Orenberg.

Towards the end of April the court returned to Cabul. Affairs were far from satisfactory, The unpopularity of the English, and even of Soojah himself, became daily more and more obvious to all observant people. The dual Government was a failure. The English, pledged not to interfere with Soojah, were obliged to permit much of which they strongly disapproved to pass unchallenged, and were only called upon to intervene to pass measures which Soojah himself was not strong enough to enforce. Whenever therefore their presence did make itself conspicuously felt it had the natural result of only increasing their unpopularity.

The expense had already been enormous, and showed no signs of decreasing. The wealth and liberality of the English had been a tradition in Afghanistan since the days of Elphinstone, and the Afghans, though they hated the infidel soldiers much, loved the *infidel* gold still more. Unfortunately, too, the dislike borne to the English by the Afghan men was not shared by the Afghan women, and the passion of jealousy, with but too good cause, was thus added to the passions of distrust and hate.

Evil news, too, came from every quarter; from the Bamean frontier on the north, from Herat on the west, from Candahar on the south, from Peshawur on the east. Macnaghten had never ceased importuning the Viceroy to sanction the restoration of Herat and Peshawur to the Afghan dominions. The Sikhs were now open in their declarations of enmity to the English, though they had refrained as yet from any actual hostilities, and Macnaghten, with considerable reason, declared there could be no safety in Afghanistan till, to use his own words, "the road through the Punjab was macadamised."

At Herat, too, Yar Mahomed, the *Vizier*, a man of boundless avarice and treachery, though living on British bounty, was openly intriguing with Persia, and had behaved with such gross and repeated insolence to our Envoy that the latter had at last left his court in disgust. But Lord Auckland, though not insensible to Macnaghten's arguments, did not dare at that time to increase either his responsibilities or his expenses, both of which were already sufficiently heavy. Grave complaints were heard from Candahar, where the old system of taxation that had made the Barukzye rule so irksome was still in force, and still in the hands of the same hated collectors.

The Ghilzyes, who had already received severe punishment from Outram, were again in the field, and further still to the south the whole country was in revolt. Khelat had been won back from us by Mehrab Khan's son, and Loveday, the English officer in charge, barbarously murdered. In the far north our outposts had pushed on over the Bamean range, and were in frequent collision with the Oosbegs, and other supporters of the Barukzye cause. It is true that wherever our troops met the enemy in the open field the victory remained with the former, but that such meetings were as frequent as they were showed the angry temper of the country but too plainly to all who had eyes to see and ears to hear.

Still the sanguine temperament of Macnaghten refused to recognise the impracticability of the game. Still he persisted in believing in the popularity of Soojah, and in the ultimate settlement of his kingdom, and as a proof of his confidence he about this time sent down to Bengal for his wife, an example which was followed by most of the other married officers.

The news from the north soon became still more alarming. Jubbar Khan was at Khooloom with the *Ameer's* family, living on the bounty of the *wullee*, or chief of that place, who still upheld with fidelity rare for an Afghan the cause of the fugitive king. Other once staunch supporters, however, had "come in," as the phrase went, among them Azim Khan, one of the *Ameer's* sons, and it was reported that Jubbar himself was vacillating. A forward movement of our troops would, it was believed, soon bring him to his senses. A forward movement was accordingly made and the *Khan* did "come in." On July 3rd he arrived at Bamean with his brother's family, and a large party of retainers.

But now the *Ameer* himself was once more in the field. At first a guest in the court of Bokhara, he had afterwards become the prisoner of that treacherous chief, who, had he dared, would have murdered his captive, and his sons with him, as he would have murdered the English Envoy. But Dost Mahomed, who as he said of himself, "was a wooden spoon, to be thrown hither and thither without hurt," contrived in some way to effect his escape, and, after infinite hardships, to make his way to his old ally of Khooloom, who welcomed him with open arms. The Oosbegs gathered to the popular standard.

The *Ameer* was reminded that his wives and children were in our power; "I have no family," was his answer, "I have buried my wives and children," and at the head of 8000 men he advanced on Bamean early in September. Our troops had been compelled to abandon the outposts they had established beyond the frontier. They had never failed indeed to repel the frequent attacks that had been made on them, but it had become at last painfully

45

evident that such isolated posts were no longer tenable. They fell back therefore to Bamean, losing everything on the retreat, and to make matters still worse a regiment of Afghan infantry that had been lately raised went over in a body to the enemy.

Meanwhile, however, Dennie had come up with strong reinforcements, and on September 18th a decisive battle was fought. The enemy were immeasurably the stronger both in numbers and position, but the victory was ours, and for the second time Dost Mahomed only escaped death by the speed of his horse. But though he saved his life, he lost a valuable friend. *Dennie's* guns had a salutary effect on the *wullee*, and within a few days of the battle the old man prudently came to terms with the English, pledging himself no longer to harbour or assist Dost Mahomed or any of his family. Great was the delight in the camp at Cabul, where affairs had begun to look very black indeed, and serious apprehensions at one time entertained of an insurrection;—but they had not yet done with the *Ameer*.

Driven out of the Hindoo Koosh, our gallant enemy next reappeared in Kohistan. a district only too ripe for revolt. Sale was ordered out to meet him and Burnes went with him, while Wade was despatched from Jellalabad to act against the refractory Wuzzeerees. After a series of small successes, in one of which Edward Conolly, a young cavalry officer of great bravery and promise, was killed, and one repulse at Joolgah, Sale, on November 2nd, met the *Ameer* at Purwandurrah, in the Nijrow country, a name disastrous among many other disastrous names in the annals of the Afghan war.

The latter had no original intention of giving battle, but a chance movement of our horse changed his mind. Lord, one of our political agents, had proposed that our cavalry, the 2nd Bengal Light Cavalry, should take up new ground on the Afghan flank. The order had been given, and the two squadrons, numbering something over two hundred sabres, had already gone "threes about," when Dost Mahomed, seeing, as he supposed, the British in retreat, rode straight down on them at the head of about 400 horsemen. Fraser, who was in command, at once

46

facing his men about, gave the order to charge, and dashed, with his officers behind him, full at the advancing squadrons.

Not a trooper followed. At an irresolute walk they met the onset, and scarcely even waiting to cross swords, fled in every direction, leaving their officers to their fate. Of these, two, Crispin and Broadfoot, were instantly cut down; Lord managed to win his way through the sabres, only to fall immediately afterwards by a shot from one of the forts; Fraser, severely wounded, was saved only by the strength and speed of his horse; how the others escaped no man could say.

Our infantry managed in a measure to retrieve the fortunes of the day. The Afghans were driven from their position, but their leader once again escaped from out our very grasp. Lawrence has generously tried to find excuses for the conduct of his men (he was not himself with them, for at that time he was acting as assistant agent to Macnaghten), but the fact remains that a native regiment, hitherto famous for its bravery and fidelity, refused to follow its English officers on the field of battle, and fled like sheep before a horde of irregular horsemen not twice their number.

Burnes wrote off to Cabul forthwith to announce, perhaps somewhat to magnify, the disaster, and implored Macnaghten to concentrate all our troops at once on the capital, in anticipation, which all then believed to be certain, of the *Ameer's* instant advance. Far other, however, were at that time the plans of Dost Mahomed. He did, indeed, advance on the capital, but attended only by a single attendant, and within twenty-four hours after his victory he had placed his sword in Macnaghten's hands.

Force would never have driven him to such a step, but he was weary of fighting in a cause which, so far as he then could foresee, could but be hopeless, and he felt that after his brilliant triumph of the previous day he could lay down his arms without disgrace. Macnaghten and the other English officers received him with the utmost courtesy, Nicholson, an officer of great bravery and intelligence, was appointed to take charge of him, but the indignity of a guard was spared him.

Soojah refused to see him, on the ground that he should be "unable to show common civility to such a villain." Many, however, who had held persistently aloof from Soojah, came to pay their respects to one whom they still regarded as their lawful ruler; one of them, Shere Mahomed, known as the swiftest mounted messenger in all Afghanistan, exclaiming, as he grasped his chief cordially by the hand, "Ah, *Ameer*, you have done right at last; why did you delay so long putting an end to all your miseries?" Within a few days the *Ameer's* son, Afzul Khan, followed his father's example, and on November 13th the two illustrious prisoners set out for India, under the charge of Nicholson and a strong escort of British troops.

As in the previous year the court passed the winter months at Jellalabad. Cotton was already there on his way down to India, "anxious to get away," and only waiting the arrival of his successor. General Elphinstone. Elphinstone was a brave, kindly, and courteous old gentleman; he had seen service in the Peninsular, and bore the Waterloo medal, but he was entirely without experience of Indian warfare; was, moreover, sadly crippled in health, and unfortunately destitute of the very qualities of energy and foresight which were peculiarly necessary to his position.

His appointment was made against his own personal inclinations, nor was it precisely clear on what grounds it had been made, save on the grounds that he was a relation of Lord Elphinstone, at that time Governor of Bombay. But he was ordered to assume the command, and, as a soldier, he obeyed his orders. Cotton handed over his charge, and took his leave with these words, "You will have nothing to do here; all is peace." Never was there made a more unfortunate remark.

The winter passed in tolerable quiet, but with the return of spring came back the old troubles. The first symptoms of disquiet appeared again in the neighbourhood of Candahar. Two admirable officers were in charge there, Nott and Rawlinson, the former holding the military, the latter the political command. The irrepressible Ghilzyes were again in revolt, and the Douranees had risen to join them. Soojah was particularly eager to conciliate the latter tribe, and had, when at Candahar, remitted many of the impositions which had rendered the Barukzye rule so odious; but he had also, as has been already said, retained in office the equally odious tax-collectors who had been employed under the latter dynasty, and the Douranees, anticipating complete redress, and probably substantial rewards, were irritated past endurance to find their state no better under their own king than it had been under the usurper.

Long ripe for revolt, their disaffection had been secretly fomented by that indefatigable traitor the Herat *Vizier*, Yar Mahomed, whose intrigues found a willing tool in Aktur Khan, a chief of the Zemindawer country. Rawlinson, anxious to try the effect of conciliatory measures, and believing with Burnes that Afghanistan was not to be settled at the point of the bayonet, despatched his assistant Elliot to confer with the insurgents. The mission was successful for the time; Aktur Khan "came in;" certain concessions were made, and certain honours conferred upon him, in return for which he promised to disband his followers.

But the peace, as Rawlinson anticipated, was short-lived. The gallant but imprudent conduct of Lynch, our political agent among the Ghilzye tribes, in storming a small fort near Khelat-i-Ghilzye, to avenge an insult offered him by the garrison, had set that turbulent country in a flame. Wymer was sent out by Nott to settle matters, which he did effectively enough. The Ghilzyes, under a famous leader known as the "*Gooroo,*" fought like madmen, holding our troops in check for five fierce hours; but they gave way at last, and fled, leaving the greater part of their number dead or dying on the field.

Aktur Khan, fired by the example, scattered his promises to the winds, and instead of disbanding, collected anew his forces for another struggle. Woodburn, a dashing officer, met him on the banks of the Helmund, and defeated him after a smart engagement, but the British forces were insufficient to follow up the victory, and on reaching Ghiresk Woodburn was compelled to await the arrival of more troops from Candahar. Thence, strongly reinforced, he moved out on August 17th, and after a short but sharp struggle, in which the *Janbaz*, or Afghan Horse, for once in a way behaved with great gallantry, Aktur Khan fled, completely routed, and for a time again there was peace among the Douranees.

The Ghilzyes, too, at the same time had received so severe a repulse from Chambers, that even they were forced to abstain from action for a while, and the dreaded "*Gooroo*" was at last prevailed on to "come in" to the English camp. On the north-western frontier our troops had been equally successful under Nott and Wymer. Akrum Khan, a close ally of Aktur Khan, was in arms in the Dehrawut country, and would submit neither to promises, threats, nor force. Treachery, however, did its work at last. One of his own countrymen offered to betray him, and by a rapid night march the rebel was seized, and carried down a close prisoner to Candahar.

Macnaghten, at times humane almost to a fault, had at length resolved to give a terrible example to these continued disturbers of the public peace. Orders were sent down to Prince Timour, who governed for his father at Candahar, and who would have obeyed any orders emanating from his English allies, and Akrum Khan was blown from a gun. By the end of October, 1841, there at last seemed really a prospect of peace in Western Afghanistan.

Despite the warnings of Rawlinson, who could see farther below the surface than most of his comrades, and who knew well that there was something more than mere discontent at an obnoxious tax lurking in the hearts of the western tribes— despite, too, the shadow of Akbar Khan, Dost Mahomed's favourite son, who was still hovering about our northern frontier— Macnaghten's spirits rose higher than they had ever risen before. Of a temperament peculiarly susceptible to the influence of the hour, he was alternately depressed and exalted beyond reason, as the varying fortunes of our arms favoured or threatened the ultimate success of his plans.

After the disaster of Purwandurrah he was convinced that the game was lost; after the discomfiture of the Ghilzyes and the death of Akrum Khan he was equally convinced that the game was won, and in one of his letters, written about this time to a private friend, he boasted that the country was quiet "from Dan to Beersheba." The well-earned reward of his labours had come at last in the shape of the Government of Bombay; within a few weeks he hoped to turn his back on the scene of so many anxieties and so many disappointments, leaving to his successor the legacy of an accomplished task.

That successor would of course be Burnes; Burnes, who had a clearer eye for the future than his chief, and who felt in his inmost heart that the end of such a system as had been established in Afghanistan could not be far off, yet who, impatient for Macnaghten's departure, was willing to dare all risks, so that he might at last touch the goal of his ambition. And at this very time, in that serene sky, the cloud was gathering that was to break when least expected, and overwhelm Macnaghten and Burnes and the whole English cause in utter ruin.

Elphinstone, as has been said, was now in command of the British forces. Next in rank to him were Sir Robert Sale, of the 13th Light Infantry, and Brigadier Shelton, who had come up in the spring of the year with his regiment, the 44th of the Line. Soojah's own troops were under Brigadier Anquetil, who had superseded Roberts, much to Macnaghten's satisfaction, for Roberts was too much of an "alarmist" to please the sanguine envoy. The main body of the garrison lay in the new cantonments.

These remarkable works had been erected in the previous year. Situated in low, swampy ground about two miles from the citadel, they were defended only by a low mud rampart and ditch, over which a pony had been ridden for a wager by one of our own officers; they were commanded on every side by hills and villages, while, to make matters still worse, the commissariat supplies were stored in a small fort without the wall. The authority for this unfortunate arrangement has been the subject of much discussion, into which it would be neither profitable nor pleasant to enter here; but it should not, at least, be forgotten that our engineer officers had always urged most strongly the expediency of posting the troops in the Bala Hissar, or citadel, a strong position on a hill commanding the entire city and suburbs.

At first, indeed, this had been done, but the soldiers were soon required to give way to the ladies of Soojah's *harem*, and it was then deemed necessary, by some person or persons, to build what Kaye aptly calls "the sheep-folds on the plain." Elphinstone, at any rate, was not to blame, whoever was, for the folly had been committed before Elphinstone had assumed the command.

But familiarity, as usual, soon begot security, and in this dangerous position our officers and men soon learned to live as tranquilly and easily as in the strongest fortress in the world, or as in the luxurious quarters they had left in peaceful Hindostan. The time passed pleasantly enough. Lady Macnaghten and Lady Sale, (*Lady Sale's Afghanistan* by Florentia Sale also published by Leonaur), had joined their husbands, and nearly all the married officers had followed the example of their chiefs. The climate was fine and bracing, nor was there any lack either of amusement or society.

Englishmen carry their sports with them into every quarter of the globe, and the stolid Afghans looked in amazement and admiration on the races, the cricket, and the skating with which the white-faced infidels beguiled the idle days. But there were unfortunately other habits in which some of the English chose to indulge which stirred up in the native heart feelings of a very different nature, habits which have already been briefly touched upon, and which were growing fast into an open and notorious scandal. "There are many," wrote Kaye in 1851, "who can fill in with vivid personality all the melancholy details of this chapter of human weakness, and supply a catalogue of the wrongs which were soon to be so fearfully redressed."

Macnaghten proposed to set his face towards home in November. His last days, as ill-fortune would have it, had been again embittered with revolt, arising from an unpopular measure which he had felt himself obliged to sanction. Our sojourn in Afghanistan had been a fearful drain on the resources of the Indian Government, and the need for economy had been urgently pressed upon Lord Auckland by the authorities at home. Macnaghten, casting about for the means of obeying his chief's instructions, unluckily hit upon the most unfortunate means he could have chosen.

He determined to inaugurate a general system of retrenchment in the stipends, or subsidies, paid to the chiefs, and as a beginning, the sum of £3000, which had been yearly paid to the Eastern Ghilzyes to secure our communications with Hindostan, was forthwith stopped. As a natural result they at once flew to arms, occupied the passes on the road to Jellalabad, commenced an organised system of plundering, and entirely cut off the communications it was our greatest interest to keep open. But the envoy was not very seriously disturbed. Sale's brigade, which was under orders for India, could "thresh the rascals" on its homeward journey, and clear the passes easily enough. Monteith was accordingly sent out with the 35th Native Infantry, a squadron of cavalry, and some guns, and Sale followed with his own regiment, the 13th Light Infantry.

The task was not so easy as the envoy had anticipated. Sale himself was wounded and Wyndham, of the 35th, killed. It was found necessary to despatch more troops before the work could be done. It was done, however, partly by force and partly by diplomacy; the Khoord-Cabul defile was once more cleared; detachments of troops were posted at intervals along the pass, while Sale himself, halting at Gundamuck, put away his ideas of home for a time.

November 1st was the day fixed for Macnaghten's departure. He was not without warnings that for some days past there had existed strong symptoms of disaffection in the city, where the shopkeepers were closing their shutters, and refusing to sell their wares to the English. John Conolly, a relative of the Envoy's, had got an inkling of what was meditated, while Mohun Lal, an interpreter, who had served us faithfully from the time of our first entry into the country, had directly warned Burnes of a conspiracy of which Abdoolah Khan, one of our most uncompromising opponents, was the prime instigator, and in which the chiefs of all the tribes then assembled in Cabul were alike implicated. But Burnes was still under the orders of Macnaghten, and Macnaghten still refused to listen to the "croakers." On that very evening the conspirators met for the last time, and on the morning of the 2nd the city rose in insurrection.

Burnes himself was the first victim. His house was within the city walls, next to that of Captain Johnson, the paymaster of Soojah's troops. On the previous night Johnson had slept in the cantonments, but Burnes was at home, and with him his brother Charles, and William Broadfoot, an able officer, who had been selected by the expectant Envoy for the post of military secretary. Before daybreak he had again been warned of his danger by a friendly native, and at a later hour came Osman Khan, the *Vizier* himself, with the same tale, imploring him to seek safety either in the citadel or the cantonments. Burnes could no longer disbelieve, for already an angry crowd was gathering under his windows, and angry voices were raised in clamour for the lives of the Englishmen.

He consented to write to the envoy for aid, and to send messengers to Abdoolah Khan, promising him that if he would restrain the citizens his grievances should receive prompt redress. Why no immediate answer was returned to the first of these messages has never been made perfectly clear; the latter resulted only in the death of the messenger. Meanwhile Burnes himself was haranguing the mob from an upper gallery, while his brother and the guard were firing on them from below. In vain he appealed to their avarice; the only answer was that he should "come down into the garden."

A Cashmerian, who had found his way into the house, swore to pass him and his brother out in safety to the cantonments, if the latter would bid the firing cease. Hastily disguising themselves, the brothers followed the man to the door, but scarcely had they set foot beyond it, when the traitor shouted with a loud voice, "This is Sekunder Burnes!" In a moment the mob were on them, and, hacked to pieces by the cruel Afghan knives, then fell the first, but not the last victims of a long series of mistakes.

The paymaster's house was next sacked; upwards of £17,000 of the public money and £1000 of Johnson's private fortune fell to the share of the murderers. No force came from the cantonments to check them, and the only effort made in the early part of the day was made by Soojah himself, who sent one of his own regiments down from the Bala Hissar into the city. Entangled in a network of narrow lanes and bazaars, they could do no good, and Shelton, coming up later with a small body of infantry and artillery, was in time only to cover a disorderly flight.

It is difficult to decide on the true cause of the lateness of Shelton's arrival, but it is certain that had Burnes's message received prompt attention, the insurrection, for that time at least, would have been nipped in the bud. That such was the opinion of the Afghans themselves many of our officers were subsequently assured, and the fact that none of the chief conspirators took any part in the first outbreak seems to give colour to the supposition that it was not the original design to proceed to such extremities as followed, but rather to convey to the British such a warning as might convince them of the hopelessness of their cause, and induce them at last to take measures to leave the country to its own devices.

Be this, however, as it may, nothing was done till the time had passed for anything to be of use, and a riot which 300 resolute men could have quelled with ease in the morning, would in the afternoon have taxed, if not defied, the best energies of 3000.

The history of the days which followed between the first rising and the opening of negotiations is as difficult to write as it is painful to read. So many and so conflicting are the accounts that have been received, that it is impossible within a limited space to present a distinct and coherent narrative of events, or, without the risk of a hasty conclusion, to apportion, even were it desirable to do so, the precise share of responsibility to each actor in that dismal tragedy of errors. It is certain, at least, that from the

2nd to the 25th November the utmost confusion and dismay prevailed within the British cantonments.

No two of the authorities seem ever to have counselled alike; there was disunion between Elphinstone and Macnaghten, and disunion even between Elphinstone and Shelton. Orders were issued one hour to be countermanded the next, and then re-issued. There was no lack of individual boldness in council, and, among the officers, no lack of individual bravery in action, but want of co-operation rendered both alike useless. Our strength was frittered away in a series of petty sorties, conducted by insufficient numbers, and generally ordered when the time for immediate action was past.

Our soldiers, even our own English soldiers, disheartened and demoralized by repeated defeats, for which they felt that they themselves were not to blame, lost confidence alike in their commanders and in themselves. It is said that it was actually found necessary to employ a *Sepoy* guard to prevent the soldiers of an English regiment leaving their post, and it is certain that on one, if not on more than one occasion, our men fairly turned their backs and ran before the Afghan hordes.

At an early day, as might well have been foreseen, the forts containing the commissariat supplies and stores fell into the enemy's hands, and though this disaster was for a time remedied by the energies of our commissariat officers, who had fortunately not been lost with the stores, and who managed to collect supplies from some of the neighbouring villages, there soon arose a new danger in the doubt whether the siege would not outlast the ammunition.

Urgent and frequent messages had been sent to bring up Sale's brigade, which was supposed to be still among the Khoord-Cabul hills, and to Eldred Pottinger to join the garrison with his detachment from Charekur, a place about 60 miles north of Cabul. But Sale's brigade was already on its march to Jellalabad, and of Pottinger's detachment only he and another officer reached Cabul alive. To crown all, it was known that Akbar Khan was moving down from Bamean.

On the 23rd a strong force of cavalry and infantry, but accompanied, through what strange process of reasoning it is impossible to say, by only one gun, moved out under Shelton to occupy a hill commanding the sources of our supplies, which had been recently threatened by the enemy. The expedition was a total failure.

Shelton himself behaved with conspicuous gallantry, and his officers nobly followed his example; but the men, discouraged by frequent defeat, and finding their muskets no match for the Afghan *jezails*, were mown down like grass, till, having lost their solitary piece of artillery, they fled in disgraceful panic back to the cantonments. With this disastrous attempt concluded all exterior operations, and on the same day Macnaghten received instructions from Elphinstone to open negotiations for surrender.

At the first meeting the terms offered were so insulting that Macnaghten refused to continue the conference. His hopes, too, had somewhat revived of late by a communication from Mohun Lal, whom he had secretly employed to sow, with offers of large bribes, dissensions among the hostile chiefs, and by the news of the death of two of our bitterest foes, Abdoolah Khan and Meer Musjedee. Whether these men died from wounds received in battle, or by assassins set on by Mohun Lal, is not certain, but it seems tolerably clear that the interpreter was instigated by someone in the British camp to offer large sums of money for the heads of the principal insurgents.

As a set-off to this, however, came grave reports from the Commissariat department, and the news that there was little prospect of Maclaren's brigade, which had set out from Candahar to their relief, being able to win its way to Cabul. On December 11th, therefore, negotiations were renewed. Akbar Khan, who had by this time joined his countrymen amid uproarious expressions of delight, with the chiefs of all the principal tribes, met the Envoy on the banks of the Cabul River, about a mile from the cantonments.

Macnaghten read in Persian the draft treaty he had prepared, of which the main stipulations were to the following effect:—

That the British troops in Afghanistan should be withdrawn to India as speedily as possible, accompanied by two *Sirdars* of rank as guarantees of safe conduct; that on their arrival at Peshawur arrangements should at once be made for the return of Dost Mahomed and all others of his countrymen at that time detained in India; that Soojah should be allowed to depart with the troops, or to remain where he was on a suitable provision, as he might prefer; and that four "respectable" British officers were to be left at Cabul as hostages for the due fulfilment of the treaty until the return of Dost Mahomed and his family.

After a discussion of two hours the terms were accepted, and it was agreed that the evacuation of our position should commence in three days' time. Such a treaty is not to be read with pleasure, but it was possibly the best that could have been concluded under the circumstances that had arisen; for which Macnaghten himself appears, at least, to have been less responsible than his military colleagues, at whose urgent and repeated instigations he had undertaken the work.

It became soon apparent how little dependence was to be placed on the Afghan word. On the 13th, according to the stipulation, the British troops stationed in the citadel left their quarters, about six o'clock on a winter's evening. Scarcely had they cleared the gates, when an ugly rush was made for them by the crowd outside. The gates were immediately closed, and the guns of the citadel opened an indiscriminate fire on friends and foes alike. Akbar Khan declared that at that late hour he could not undertake their safe conduct to the cantonments, and the men were therefore obliged to pass the night on the frosty ground, without tents, without food, and without fuel.

On the following morning they reached the cantonments in safety, but half-dead with hunger and exposure. It had been agreed that the Afghans should supply the necessary provisions and carriage for the march; but it had also been agreed that the British forts in the neighbourhood of their position should be given up. The Afghans refused to play their part till we had played ours, and the forts were accordingly placed in their hands.

Still, provisions came in but slowly, and carriage not at all. A horde of robbers and fanatics swarmed between the city and the cantonments, plundering under our very eyes the few supplies that were sent in, but as they were now to be considered "as our allies" not a shot was permitted to be fired.

Yet even then Macnaghten continued to hope against hope, that "something might turn up" to spare the humiliation of an enforced retreat, and on the evening of the 22nd it seemed to him that such a chance had arrived. It came in the shape of a proposal from Akbar Khan that he and the Ghilzyes should, in the face of the concluded treaty, unite with the English to reoccupy the citadel and the abandoned forts; that our forces should be allowed to remain in Afghanistan till the spring, and then withdraw as though of their own free-will; that the head of the formidable Ameen-oolah Khan should be sent to the envoy, and that in consideration of all these good offices Akbar Khan himself should receive an annuity of four *lakhs* of *rupees* from the British Government, together with a bonus of thirty *lakhs*.

The offer of murder was indignantly rejected, but with the others Macnaghten closed at once, and on the following morning, having requested that two regiments with some guns might be held ready for instant service, he rode out to the proposed place of conference, accompanied by Lawrence, Trevor and Mackenzie. The latter, indeed, learning the new design, ventured to expostulate with his chief on the risk he was about to run, while Elphinstone earnestly implored him to pause before he committed himself to so perilous and so crooked a course; but despising warnings and advice alike, Macnaghten rode hopefully out to his death.

Among some small hillocks about 600 yards from the cantonments the meeting was appointed; salutations were exchanged, the party dismounted, and the envoy and the *Khan* seated themselves on the ground. Scarcely had the conversation been opened, when the chiefs began to close in on the little group. It was pointed out to Akbar that as the conference was a secret one, they should be advised to withdraw; he answered that it was of no matter, as they were all in the plot with him.

The words had not left his lips when the Englishmen were seized. Trevor, Lawrence and Mackenzie were flung each behind a mounted Afghan and galloped off to one of the forts, through a crowd of armed fanatics, who cut and struck at them as they passed. On the way Trevor slipped from his seat and was instantly hacked to pieces, but the others got safely through. As they were hurried away, Lawrence turned his head and saw the envoy struggling in the grasp of Akbar Khan, "with an awful look of horror and consternation on his face;" a pistol shot was heard soon after, and no English eye ever saw Macnaghten alive or dead again. Such was the end of the attempt of an honest Englishman to outwit the most treacherous people in the world.

On the following day new terms were sent to Elphinstone to be added to the existing treaty—that first treaty which Macnaghten had lost his life in attempting to evade. These required that the guns with the exception of six, and all the muskets, save those in actual use, should be given up, and that the numbers of hostages should be increased. Eldred Pottinger, who had succeeded to the envoy's place, strongly combated this additional insult, giving his undaunted voice for the immediate seizure of the citadel, or at least for one last attempt to fight their way sword in hand down to Jellalabad.

His brave counsel was overruled; the guns and muskets were given up, a few at a time, in the vain hope that in some way the treaty might yet be averted, or perhaps to alleviate, if possible, the humiliation of the surrender; Captains Walsh and Drummond, with Lieutenants Warburton and Webb were sent to join Lieutenants Conolly and Airy, who were already in the hands of the chiefs, and such of the sick and wounded as were unable to bear the fatigues of the march were conveyed into the city under Doctors Berwick and Campbell. On the 6th of January, 1842, before the promised escorts had arrived, the British army, contrary again to Pottinger's advice, moved out from the cantonments, and the fatal march began.

The British troops that marched out on that 6th January

numbered 4,500 fighting men, of whom 700 were Europeans, and about 12,000 camp followers. Of this force two men reached Jellalabad alive, one of whom died on the following day.

The married officers and their wives, with all the women and children, and a few of the wounded, were on the third day of the retreat placed in the care of Akbar Khan, who, to give him such credit as is his due, for once kept his word when he promised to treat them honourably and well; six more officers, including the General himself and Shelton, at a later period fell or were surrendered as hostages, into the same hands, and were carried back up country, though Elphinstone, sick in body as in heart, prayed hard to be allowed to die with his men; Captain Souter, of the 44th, who had wrapped the regimental colours round his waist, was taken prisoner with a few private soldiers at Gundamuck, where the last stand was made by the gallant handful who had survived the horrors of the pass.

The rest of the Europeans perished to a man beneath the knives and bullets of their "allies." Among the Native troops and camp followers the loss was probably less than was at the time, and has been generally since, supposed. Some of the former deserted in sheer terror to the Afghans, and some of the latter it is possible found hiding-places among the mountains, whence, when the noise of battle had passed on, they contrived to make good their escape; yet thousands fell beneath the murderous rain that poured down night and day upon the defenceless rabble, and thousands, untouched by shot or steel, from utter weariness sank down into the snow to rise no more.

Had the march been pushed on from the first with more expedition, it is probable that at least a far larger number would have been saved; but that, owing to the general demoralisation that had set in, inspired by the irresolution of the commander, and aggravated by the disorderly crowd of camp-followers, whose terror quenched all notions of discipline, was precisely what could not be done.

From dawn vast hordes of *Ghazee* fanatics had hung on the rear, cutting off stragglers, plundering the baggage, and from every coign of vantage firing indiscriminately into the struggling line. The roads were slippery with ice, and on the evening of the first day the snow began to fall; on the second day the march became but "a rabble in chaotic rout."

The European troops indeed, set a glorious example. The officers did all that mortals could do to preserve discipline, and the men, obeying so far as it was possible to obey, nobly redeemed their former errors; but hampered by a helpless crowd whose one thought of safety was not to fight but to fly, it was but little that they could do. Here and there a stand was made by gallant handfuls of our men, and where the English stood, there the Afghans fled, but these momentary triumphs served rather to increase than to check the fury of our foes. Enough of a melancholy and shameful tale—let it be sufficient to say that when Brydon reached Jellalabad on the 13th the army of Cabul had for all practical purposes disappeared from off the face of the earth.

The news came upon the Government like a thunder-stroke. The last days of Lord Auckland's administration were drawing near, and as he read Macnaghten's sanguine despatches he fondly hoped that it would be his fortune to return to England, not only the conqueror, but the tranquilizer of Afghanistan. Towards the close of the year, indeed, rumours of a disquieting nature had found their way down to Calcutta, and when all rumours ceased it became evident that our communications were interrupted, and that something serious had happened; but not even the gloomiest dared to anticipate the worst: on January 30th the worst was known.

Though there was anything but unanimity in the Calcutta Council, some preparations, chiefly through the energetic representations of George Clerk, our agent on the north-western frontier, had been made before the full tidings of the disaster came down. It had appeared to some, of whom was Sir Jasper Nicolls, then commander-in-chief in India, that it was better to accept the blow, and withdraw altogether behind the Indus, than by attempting to retrieve still further to deepen our disgrace. Sale still held Jellalabad in the teeth of overwhelming numbers; Nott was still master of Candahar;—let them yield up the charge they had so nobly kept, and if too weak to find their own way down to India, let troops sufficient for their help advance, but for no other purpose.

Lord Auckland, unwilling to commit his successor to a task which had already proved too strong for his own energies, was inclined to listen to the advocates of retreat, and though the news of the annihilation of the army of Cabul roused him for the moment into a proclamation that the awful calamity was but "a new occasion for displaying the stability and vigour of the British power, and the admirable spirit and valour of the British-Indian army," he quickly followed it by an intimation that when Sale and Nott had been relieved it were better that the British troops should withdraw to Peshawur. Still, fresh forces were to be raised, and a fine soldier was to head them.

The offer had been first made to Major-General Lumley, Adjutant-General in India, but Lumley's health forbade him to accept so important a post, and Lord Auckland's choice—a choice as popular as it was judicious—finally fell upon Pollock, a distinguished officer of the Company's service, who had seen fighting under Lake and Wellington, and wherever, indeed, it was to be seen since the year 1803, when he had first landed in India, a young lieutenant of artillery. Pollock hastened up to his command without a moment's delay, but before he could reach Peshawur our troops had suffered yet another repulse.

Mr. Robertson, Lieutenant-Governor of the north western frontier, and George Clerk, already mentioned, had counselled from the first prompt measures, not of retreat, but reprisal. At their earnest request Colonel Wild had been moved up to Peshawur with four native infantry regiments, the 30th, 53rd, 60th and 64th, but without guns. It was supposed he could procure them from the Sikhs, and with a great deal of trouble he did manage to procure four rickety guns, which seemed likely to do as much harm to his own men as to the enemy, and one of which broke down the next day on trial. Reinforcements were coming up, which it was probable would contain artillery, but Wild did not dare to wait. His *Sepoys* were anxious to advance; the loyalty of the Sikhs was doubtful, and he feared the contamination might spread. On January 15th he commenced operations.

The key of the Khyber Pass, as we have all heard more than once within the last few weeks, is the fortress of Ali Musjid, occupying a strong position some five miles down the pass, and about twenty-five from Peshawur. It had been recently garrisoned by some loyal natives under an English officer, Mackeson; but, straitened for provisions, and hard pressed by the Khyberees, it was doubtful whether the brave little garrison could hold out much longer, and on the night of the 15th the 53rd and 64th Regiments, under Colonel Moseley, were despatched with a goodly supply of bullocks to its relief.

The fort was occupied without loss, but the bullocks, save some 50 or 60, had meanwhile disappeared, and there were now more mouths to feed in Ali Musjid and less wherewith to feed them. Wild was to have followed with the other two regiments, his Sikh guns and Sikh allies, on the 19th, but when the time came the latter turned their backs on the Khyber and marched to a man back to Peshawur. The *Sepoys* met the enemy at the mouth of the pass, but the spirit of disaffection seemed to have spread.

After an irresolute and aimless volley they halted in confusion: in vain Wild and his officers called on them to advance; not a man moved; the guns broke down, and one of them, despite the gallant efforts of Henry Lawrence, had to be abandoned. One of our officers was killed, and Wild himself, with several more, was wounded; the retreat was sounded, and the column fell back on Jumrood. The two regiments which held the fort had soon to follow their example. They could have held the post for any time indeed, so far as mere fighting went, but they had no provisions, and the water was poisonous.

On the 23rd, then, they evacuated their position, and after a sharp struggle, in which two English officers fell, and some sick and baggage had to be abandoned, made good their way back to their comrades. Such was the state of affairs Pollock found on his arrival at Peshawur.

Despite urgent letters received from Jellalabad the General saw that an immediate advance was impossible. The morale of the defeated *Sepoys* had fallen very low; the hospitals were crowded with sick and wounded, and there was still an insufficiency of guns. Reinforcements of British dragoons and British artillery were pressing up from the Punjab, and Pollock decided to wait till he could make certain of success. He decided well; nor was the time of waiting lost. He visited the hospitals daily, cheering the sick, and reanimating by his kindness and decision the wavering and disheartened *Sepoys*. On March 30th the long-desired reinforcements arrived, and orders were at once issued for the advance.

At three o'clock on the morning of April 5th the army moved off from Jumrood to the mouth of the pass. It was divided into three columns; two of these were to crown the heights on either side, while the third, when the hills had been sufficiently cleared, was to advance through the gorge; each column was composed of a mixed force of Europeans and *Sepoys*; four squadrons of the 3rd Dragoons and eleven pieces of artillery accompanied the centre column. The attack was as successful as it was ingenious. A huge barricade of mud and stones and trunks of trees had been thrown across the mouth of the pass, while the heights on either side swarmed with the wild hill-tribes.

So quietly, however, did our flanking columns advance, that they were half-way up the heights before the enemy became aware of the movement. From peak to peak our men, English as well as *Sepoys*, clambered as agile as the mountaineers themselves, pouring from every spot of vantage a steady and well-directed fire on the disconcerted Khyberees, who had never dreamed that the white-faced *infidels* could prove more than a match for them in their own fastnesses.

Then Pollock with the main column advanced. The Afghans, finding themselves out-flanked on either side, gradually withdrew; the barricade was removed without loss; and the huge line of soldiers, camp-followers, and baggage-waggons passed unopposed on its victorious way to Jellalabad. The dreaded Khyber Pass had been forced with the slightest possible loss of life, and the boastful Afghans beaten at their own tactics.

On the 16th Jellalabad was reached. With what intense delight Sale's noble brigade saw once more from their walls the colours of a friendly force may well be imagined. For five weary months the little band had resisted every offer of surrender, and beaten back every assault. In February the fortifications that had been raised and strengthened by Broadfoot with infinite labour were destroyed by an earthquake; and at that very time they learnt that Akbar Khan was advancing on them.

The works, however, were restored, and in a dashing sortie, commanded by Dennie, the Afghan chief, with the flower of the Barukzye Horse, was driven from his position without the loss of a single man to the garrison. A few days before Pollock arrived a still more daring enterprise had been attempted. On April 5th another sortie in force was sent out under Dennie, Monteith, and Havelock, which bore down on the Afghan camp, and sent Akbar Khan flying with his 6000 men far away in the direction of Lughman—a dashing exploit, and a complete victory, but dearly won, for it was won at the cost of the gallant Dennie.

The meeting between the two armies was, wrote Pollock to a friend, "a sight worth seeing;" according to Mr. Gleig the band of the 13th went out to play the relieving force in, and the entry was performed to the tune of "*Oh, but ye've been lang o' coming.*"

Still there was plenty yet to be done, if only the English soldiers might be allowed to do it. At first it seemed doubtful whether Lord Ellenborough, who had succeeded Lord Auckland in February, would be more willing to sanction a forward movement than was his predecessor. On his first landing, no one could have been more eager than he to avenge the humiliation of Cabul, but as he went up the country his opinions began to suffer a change. Soojah had been murdered about the very time that the Khyber Pass was forced, by the treachery of a son of

Zemaun Khan (a faithful friend to the English, by whose good offices the English captives were still living in safety, if not in comfort); his son Futteh Jung had been nominally appointed to succeed him, but his government was no more than a farce.

Jealous of each other, and jealous particularly of the rising power of Akbar Khan, it was plain that the Afghan *Sirdars* would never rest till the strength and popularity of Dost Mahomed was once more among them to restore and maintain order. Was it not better to accept the inevitable, to withdraw our troops, now that it could be done with comparative honour, and to leave the country to its own king and its own devices?

It was doubtful how much longer the brave Nott could maintain himself in Candahar, and the force that had been sent out from Sindh under England to relieve him had been beaten back at the Kojuck Pass; Ghuznee, after a stubborn resistance, had fallen, and the British officers sent prisoners to Cabul. Lord Ellenborough cannot be blamed for hesitating at such a crisis; but the urgent prayers of Pollock, Nott, and Outram at last prevailed, and orders were given that the military commanders might use their own discretion, while they were at the same time warned that failure meant the inevitable fall of the British Empire in the East.

The responsibility was gladly taken, and the advance commenced which was to retrieve, as far as it was possible to retrieve, the shame of all former failure. The advance was an unbroken series of victories. England, reinforced with some British troops, had moved out again from Quettah, cleared the Kojuck Pass, and joined Nott at Candahar. With a force now raised to a strength equal to that which lay at Jellalabad, Nott, resolute to "retire to India" by way of Ghuznee and Cabul, lost no time in setting to work.

Dividing his troops, he took with him the 40th and 41st Regiments of the Line, and the "beautiful *Sepoy*" Regiments that had stood by him so well, and despatched the rest back to India in charge of England, in whose hands also he placed Prince Timour, whom, after his father's death it was alike dangerous to take to Cabul or to leave at Candahar. About the same time Pollock, with 8000 men of all arms, including the 31st Regiment of the Line and the 3rd Dragoons, moved out from Jellalabad on the Khoord-Cabul Pass, that bloodstained theatre of an awful tragedy.

The enemy were in force at Jugdulluck, but Pollock, employing the same tactics that had been so efficacious among the Khyber hills, sent out flanking parties to clear the heights, while from below his guns kept up a hot fire of shells on their position. The Ghilzyes fought bravely, but they could not stand against the English troops in open fight, and with as little loss as in his first engagement Pollock led his men into the pass. Seven miles within, in the little valley of Tezeen, Akbar Khan, with 16,000 of his best troops, resolved to make one last throw for victory. He threw and lost.

While the English Dragoons met and broke the charge of the Afghan horse, the English infantry, gallantly seconded by the *Sepoys* and Ghoorkahs, pressed up the heights under a heavy fire. Sale himself led the advanced column; Monteith and Broadfoot and McCaskill followed. Not a shot was fired by the stormers; thick and fast flew the bullets among them from the long Afghan *jazails*, but not an English musket answered. The work was done with the bayonet, and driven from crag to crag by that "beautiful weapon" alone, the enemy fled in confusion, till amid the ringing cheers of the whole British force the British flag waved on the highest pinnacle of the pass.

This was Akbar Khan's last attempt; leaving his troops to shift for themselves, he fled northward to the Ghoreebund Valley; Pollock, over the crumbling skeletons of the comrades whom he had so worthily avenged, led his men in triumph to Cabul, and the British ensign once more flew from the heights of the Bala Hissar.

On September 15th Pollock reached Cabul, and on the 17th he was joined by Nott. After a slight check to the cavalry of his advanced guard, at an early period of his march, the latter's success had been as complete as Pollock's. At Ghoaine he had utterly routed a superior force of the enemy under Shumshood-een Khan. Ghuznee had been evacuated before even our prepa-rations for the assault were completed; the works were disman-tled and blown up, the town and citadel fired, and the famous sandal-wood "gates of Somnauth," which, according to Afghan tradition, had adorned their famous Sultan's tomb for upwards of eight centuries, carried off in accordance with Lord Ellenbor-ough's expressed desire.

At Syderabad, where in the previous November Woodburn and his men had been treacherously massacred, Shumshoodeen turned again; the stand was stubborn and for a while the is-sue seemed doubtful; but the news of the defeat at Tezeen had spread, the Afghans lost heart, and abandoning their position left the way for Nott clear into Cabul.

The honour of the British arms was at last complete; 15,000 British troops were encamped in the Afghan capital, and from every quarter round submission was pouring in. Ameen-oollah Khan, who held out to the last, had been utterly routed in the Kohistan by a force under McCaskill, and Akbar Khan had also intimated his wish to treat for terms.

The miserable Futteh Jung, who had already once been forced to fly for his life, was formally installed on his throne, but as formally warned that he was to expect no further aid or protection. The prospect before him was too much for his weak and timorous mind, and, in truth, it was far from a pleasant one; after a few days' nominal rule, he voluntarily resigned a crown which he would never have been able to keep, and Shahpoor, a high-spirited young boy of the Suddozye House, was seated in his stead.

Two things had yet to be done. The captives were to be re-covered, and some unmistakeable mark of British retribution was to be stamped on Cabul.

Before Akbar Khan took the field for the last time he had despatched all the English hostages, together with the prison-ers from Ghuznee, towards the Bamean frontier, under Saleh Mohamed. Pollock immediately on reaching Cabul had sent Sir

Richmond Shakespeare, with a party of horse in hot haste after them, and subsequently a stronger force under Sale. Before, however, the rescue arrived the prisoners had effected their own deliverance through the medium of Saleh Mohamed's cupidity.

On a promise, duly drawn up and signed by Pottinger, Lawrence and three others, of a heavy bribe, the Afghan had consented to escort them not to Turkestan and slavery, as had been intended, but back to the English camp, and it was at Kaloo, on their way down to Cabul, that, after more than eight months' daily expectation of death, they once more found themselves among English friends and safe under the English flag.

Despite the many hardships and anxieties they had undergone, their health, even of the women and children, had been marvellously preserved, and their condition had, on the whole, been far better than any they could have hoped for when they exchanged the certain dangers of the retreat for the uncertain security of Akbar Khan's word. Two only of the little band that had turned their backs on the miseries of the Khoord-Cabul Pass were missing when they rode into Sale's camp, amid the cheers of the men and a salute of welcome from the guns.

John Conolly, mourned by all who knew him, had died at Cabul a few days before the march for Bamean began, and in the previous April, after Pollock's victory had heralded the triumph which was to atone for the disasters that the British arms had experienced under his command, poor Elphinstone, after days of intense suffering in body and mind, and bewailing to the last that he had not been permitted to die with his men, passed away amid the affectionate sympathy of all his fellow-prisoners. His body was sent down to Jellalabad, and there interred with military honours in the presence of his victorious successor.

To set the seal of our triumph on Cabul it was determined to destroy the great Bazaar, where the mutilated body of Macnaghten had been exposed to the insults of his murderers. It had been first intended to demolish the citadel, but the Suddozye chiefs pleaded so earnestly for this last remnant of their royalty, that Pollock consented to spare it. During two days, October

9th and 10th, the work of destruction went on, and though every precaution was taken to prevent any farther loss beyond that ordered, and particularly any excess on the part of our soldiers, many suffered, and there was much excess.

On the 11th the homeward march began. Futteh Jung had implored the safe conduct of the British from a kingdom where he was no king, and from subjects with whom his life was not worth an hour's purchase, and with him went for the second time into exile his blind old grandfather Zemaun Shah. By the Khoord-Cabul and Khyber Passes, the scenes of so much misery and such grievous humiliation, the victorious army returned in triumph to Hindostan, and ere Ferozepore was reached they heard that the last of the Suddozye line had fled, that Akbar Khan had seized the throne in trust for his father, and that Dost Mahomed himself was even then on his way through the Punjab to resume his old dominion.

And so the English army left secure on the throne of Afghanistan the dynasty they had spent so many millions of treasure and so many thousands of lives to overthrow.

LEONAUR

ALSO FROM LEONAUR
AVAILABLE IN SOFTCOVER OR HARDCOVER WITH DUST JACKET

THE FALL OF THE MOGHUL EMPIRE OF HINDUSTAN *by H. G. Keene*—By the beginning of the nineteenth century, as British and Indian armies under Lake and Wellesley dominated the scene, a little over half a century of conflict brought the Moghul Empire to its knees.

LADY SALE'S AFGHANISTAN *by Florentia Sale*—An Indomitable Victorian Lady's Account of the Retreat from Kabul During the First Afghan War.

THE CAMPAIGN OF MAGENTA AND SOLFERINO 1859 *by Harold Carmichael Wylly*—The Decisive Conflict for the Unification of Italy.

FRENCH'S CAVALRY CAMPAIGN *by J. G. Maydon*—A Special Correspondent's View of British Army Mounted Troops During the Boer War.

CAVALRY AT WATERLOO *by Sir Evelyn Wood*—British Mounted Troops During the Campaign of 1815.

THE SUBALTERN *by George Robert Gleig*—The Experiences of an Officer of the 85th Light Infantry During the Peninsular War.

NAPOLEON AT BAY, 1814 *by F. Loraine Petre*—The Campaigns to the Fall of the First Empire.

NAPOLEON AND THE CAMPAIGN OF 1806 *by Colonel Vachée*—The Napoleonic Method of Organisation and Command to the Battles of Jena & Auerstädt.

THE COMPLETE ADVENTURES IN THE CONNAUGHT RANGERS *by William Grattan*—The 88th Regiment during the Napoleonic Wars by a Serving Officer.

BUGLER AND OFFICER OF THE RIFLES *by William Green & Harry Smith*—With the 95th (Rifles) during the Peninsular & Waterloo Campaigns of the Napoleonic Wars.

NAPOLEONIC WAR STORIES *by Sir Arthur Quiller-Couch*—Tales of soldiers, spies, battles & sieges from the Peninsular & Waterloo campaingns.

CAPTAIN OF THE 95TH (RIFLES) *by Jonathan Leach*—An officer of Wellington's sharpshooters during the Peninsular, South of France and Waterloo campaigns of the Napoleonic wars.

RIFLEMAN COSTELLO *by Edward Costello*—The adventures of a soldier of the 95th (Rifles) in the Peninsular & Waterloo Campaigns of the Napoleonic wars.

LEONAUR

ALSO FROM LEONAUR
AVAILABLE IN SOFTCOVER OR HARDCOVER WITH DUST JACKET

CAPTAIN COIGNET by Jean-Roch Coignet—A Soldier of Napoleon's Imperial Guard from the Italian Campaign to Russia and Waterloo.

HUSSAR ROCCA by Albert Jean Michel de Rocca—A French cavalry officer's experiences of the Napoleonic Wars and his views on the Peninsular Campaigns against the Spanish, British And Guerilla Armies.

MARINES TO 95TH (RIFLES) by Thomas Fernyhough—The military experiences of Robert Fernyhough during the Napoleonic Wars.

LIGHT BOB by Robert Blakeney—The experiences of a young officer in H.M 28th & 36th regiments of the British Infantry during the Peninsular Campaign of the Napoleonic Wars 1804 - 1814.

WITH WELLINGTON'S LIGHT CAVALRY by William Tomkinson—The Experiences of an officer of the 16th Light Dragoons in the Peninsular and Waterloo campaigns of the Napoleonic Wars.

SERGEANT BOURGOGNE by Adrien Bourgogne—With Napoleon's Imperial Guard in the Russian Campaign and on the Retreat from Moscow 1812 - 13.

SURTEES OF THE 95TH (RIFLES) by William Surtees—A Soldier of the 95th (Rifles) in the Peninsular campaign of the Napoleonic Wars.

SWORDS OF HONOUR by Henry Newbolt & Stanley L. Wood—The Careers of Six Outstanding Officers from the Napoleonic Wars, the Wars for India and the American Civil War.

ENSIGN BELL IN THE PENINSULAR WAR by George Bell—The Experiences of a young British Soldier of the 34th Regiment 'The Cumberland Gentlemen' in the Napoleonic wars.

HUSSAR IN WINTER by Alexander Gordon—A British Cavalry Officer during the retreat to Corunna in the Peninsular campaign of the Napoleonic Wars.

THE COMPLEAT RIFLEMAN HARRIS by Benjamin Harris as told to and transcribed by Captain Henry Curling, 52nd Regt. of Foot—The adventures of a soldier of the 95th (Rifles) during the Peninsular Campaign of the Napoleonic Wars.

THE ADVENTURES OF A LIGHT DRAGOON by George Farmer & G.R. Gleig—A cavalryman during the Peninsular & Waterloo Campaigns, in captivity & at the siege of Bhurtpore, India.

ALSO FROM LEONAUR

LEONAUR

ALSO FROM LEONAUR
AVAILABLE IN SOFTCOVER OR HARDCOVER WITH DUST JACKET

THE RELUCTANT REBEL by William G. Stevenson—A young Kentuckian's experiences in the Confederate Infantry & Cavalry during the American Civil War..

BOOTS AND SADDLES by Elizabeth B. Custer—The experiences of General Custer's Wife on the Western Plains.

FANNIE BEERS' CIVIL WAR by Fannie A. Beers—A Confederate Lady's Experiences of Nursing During the Campaigns & Battles of the American Civil War.

LADY SALE'S AFGHANISTAN by Florentia Sale—An Indomitable Victorian Lady's Account of the Retreat from Kabul During the First Afghan War.

THE TWO WARS OF MRS DUBERLY by Frances Isabella Duberly—An Intrepid Victorian Lady's Experience of the Crimea and Indian Mutiny.

THE REBELLIOUS DUCHESS by Paul F. S. Dermoncourt—The Adventures of the Duchess of Berri and Her Attempt to Overthrow French Monarchy.

LADIES OF WATERLOO by Charlotte A. Eaton, Magdalene de Lancey & Juana Smith—The Experiences of Three Women During the Campaign of 1815: Waterloo Days by Charlotte A. Eaton, A Week at Waterloo by Magdalene de Lancey & Juana's Story by Juana Smith.

TWO YEARS BEFORE THE MAST by Richard Henry Dana. Jr.—The account of one young man's experiences serving on board a sailing brig—the Penelope—bound for California, between the years 1834-36.

A SAILOR OF KING GEORGE by Frederick Hoffman—From Midshipman to Captain—Recollections of War at Sea in the Napoleonic Age 1793-1815.

LORDS OF THE SEA by A. T. Mahan—Great Captains of the Royal Navy During the Age of Sail.

COGGESHALL'S VOYAGES: VOLUME 1 by George Coggeshall—The Recollections of an American Schooner Captain.

COGGESHALL'S VOYAGES: VOLUME 2 by George Coggeshall—The Recollections of an American Schooner Captain.

TWILIGHT OF EMPIRE by Sir Thomas Ussher & Sir George Cockburn—Two accounts of Napoleon's Journeys in Exile to Elba and St. Helena: Narrative of Events by Sir Thomas Ussher & Napoleon's Last Voyage: Extract of a diary by Sir George Cockburn.

www.ingramcontent.com/pod-product-compliance
Lightning Source LLC
Chambersburg PA
CBHW032025090426
42741CB00006B/733